An Overview: The Center of Excellence on Democracy, Human Rights and Governance (DRG)

User's Guide to DRG Programming

I0448205

On February 27, 2012, USAID Administrator Rajiv Shah formally launched the agency's Center of Excellence on Democracy, Human Rights and Governance (hereafter "the DRG Center"). The launch occurred just over a year after Secretary of State Hillary Clinton and USAID Administrator Rajiv Shah released the first-ever U.S. Quadrennial Diplomacy and Development Review (QDDR). The QDDR explicitly tasked USAID with establishing the DRG Center as the primary means of elevating and integrating democracy, human rights and governance within the agency's overall development portfolio.

USAID Missions and the Washington-based DRG Center have a noble and challenging mandate captured in USAID's Mission Statement: "To end extreme poverty and promote resilient, democratic societies while advancing our security and prosperity". The DRG Center has a further defined mission statement to "advance democracy, human rights and governance for the sake of political freedom, while contributing to socioeconomic progress and overall developmental resilience by integrating DRG across all sectors". The DRG Center organizes its work to achieve the three following strategic objectives: 1) Learn: Increase knowledge concerning the global advancement of DRG; 2) Serve: Improve the quality and impact of DRG technical assistance to the field; and 3) Influence: Elevate the role of DRG in key USAID, USG and multilateral strategies, policies and budgets. With a strong emphasis on rigorous learning, the DRG Center will promote and support evidence-based DRG programming.

This User's Guide to DRG Programming has been crafted to serve as a fundamental reference tool for USAID Missions and Bureaus to utilize in pursuit of advancing democracy, human rights and good governance. This Guide outlines the structure and breadth of the DRG Center's technical expertise, as well as the DC-based DRG cadre. The Guide catalogs the funding and implementing mechanisms that may be accessed through the DRG Center and other offices, and technical resources which inform DRG work. With a strong emphasis on rigorous evaluation and learning, the DRG Center is committed to promoting evidence-based policy, strategy and programming in the DRG sector.

The Agency's primary means of implementing DRG programs in "presence" countries remains in USAID Missions. In well-defined circumstances, these mechanisms may also be used in "non-presence" countries. Overall, the DRG Center's support of missions is provided through an interlinked approach that involves technical leadership, targeted field support, cadre development and training, and direct program management. Various training as well as assessment and programming tools are developed by the DRG Center to assist missions in analyzing and choosing appropriate strategies to address the DRG issues in their host countries, as well as implement Agency-wide policies.

The eight teams that comprise the DRG Center are: 1) Civil Society and Media (CSM); 2) Cross-Sectoral Programs (CSP); 3) Elections & Political Transitions (EPT); 4) Global and Regional Policy (GRP); 5) Governance and Rule of Law (GRL); 6) Human Rights (HR); 7) Learning; and 8) Strategic Planning. There are also two permanent working groups within the DRG Center, the DRG Gender Working Group and the Training and Learning Team.

*The User's Guide to DRG Programming is regularly updated and accessible on the Center of Excellence on Democracy, Human Rights and Governance intranet site at http://inside.usaid.gov/drg.

TABLE OF CONTENTS

DRG CENTER

ORGANIZATION CHART

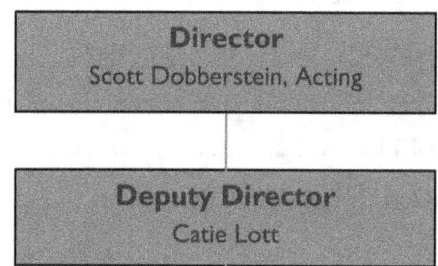

Director
Scott Dobberstein, Acting

Deputy Director
Catie Lott

Civil Society & Media
Claire Ehmann
Bama Athreya
Joshua Haynes
Patricia Hunter
Mark Koenig
Jill Moss
Maryanne Yerkes

Elections & Political Transitions
Jeffrey Vanness (Acting)
Julie Denham
Tess McEnery
Monica Moore
Assia Ivantcheva
Carol Sahley

Governance & Rule of Law
Sara Werth
Achieng Akumu
Victoria Ayer
Kenneth Barden
Colin Buckley
Adam Bushey
Keith Crawford
Mike Keshishian
Andy Michels
Keith Schulz
Julie Werbel

Human Rights
Kevin Sturr
Marina Colby
Sue Eitel
Mark Goldenbaum
Natasha Greenberg
Martin Hayes
Rob Horvath
Sandy Jenkins
Brian Keane
Vy Lam
Leah Maxson
Kristin Poore
Cathy Savino
Andrew Solomon
Nicole Widdersheim
John Williamson
Lawrence Woocher
Veronica Zeitlin

Cross-Sectoral
Laura Pavlovic
Chris Demers
Diana Cammack
Tina del Castillo
Ben Garrett
David Jacobstein
Ajit Joshi
Lisa McGregor-Mirghani
Heela Rasool
Corinne Rothblum
Sarah Swift
Lisa Williams

Global & Regional Policy
David Black
Mark Billera
Michael Bradow
Julie Browning
Bob Glover
Shannon Green
Brian Hanley
Summer Lopez
Patrick McGovern
Carrie Mitchell
Stephanie Molina

Strategic Planning
Joe Taggart
Jessica Benton Cooney
Rachel Chilton
Phyllis Daniels
Stephanie Harvey
Valerie Hovetter
Edith Koumbairia-Thomas
Virginia Leavitt
Kendra Miller
Sharon Rogers
Lauren Seyfried
Christopher White

Learning
Altin Ilirjani
Aaron Abbarno
Nicole Bonoff
Morgan Holmes
Bill Mishler

DRG CENTER TEAM AND WORKING GROUP DESCRIPTIONS

Civil Society and Media (CSM) Team

The CSM Team provides technical leadership and support on civil society (including youth, labor and media issues). The CSM Team generates comparative knowledge on effective approaches for strengthening civil society and independent media; pilots state-of-the-art approaches to civil society and media support; strengthens the agency's DRG staff through training and technical support; conducts assessments, strategy and program designs, and evaluations; and designs and manages a targeted portfolio of global programs. The CSM Team promotes innovations in the civil society, labor and media arenas (including the use of social media and other new media technologies) as a means for addressing development challenges, and represents USAID in international processes, networks and working groups.

Cross-Sectoral Programs (CSP) Team
The purpose of the CSP Team is to integrate DRG approaches and principles with other sectors. This entails working with a wide range of stakeholders as well as developing new training and learning platforms. The CSP team has staff supporting USAID Forward's Implementation and Procurement Reform (IPR) efforts, in particular Objective 1 (strengthening partner-country capacity by increasing use of reliable partner-government systems and institutions to ensure responsible and transparent use of public finances), Objective 2 (capacity development of local civil society and private sector to play a leadership role in development), and Objective 5 (building greater accountability in implementing mechanisms held by public international organizations [PIOs] towards enhanced aid effectiveness and sustainability).

Elections and Political Transitions (EPT) Team
The EPT Team provides leadership and technical assistance on political competition and consensus-building programs to USAID field Missions and Washington bureaus, other USG entities, and the broader DRG community. In doing so, the EPT Team conducts technical leadership on specific issues (including cutting-edge electoral issues) and delivers technical assistance to strengthen election administration, political parties, political finance, election monitoring and observation, voter education, and the political participation of women and marginalized groups. The EPT Team also manages the Elections and Political Processes Fund, which provides USAID Missions with funds for unanticipated electoral needs and innovative programs.

Global and Regional Policy (GRP) Team
The GRP Team supports the development and implementation of evidence-based DRG policies, strategies and budgets at the global, regional and country level. The GRP Team leads the Center's efforts in supporting country-specific DRG assessments and strategies. The team also represents the DRG sector in the Governing Justly and Democratically (GJD) budget formulation and execution process, conducting analysis and advocacy to link global and country DRG funding with needs and opportunities as well as ensuring that budget levels are consistent with core policies and strategies. Finally, the team engages within USAID and in inter-agency arenas to forge an effective link between U.S. diplomacy, policy, and programs regarding the promotion of DRG. Given the cross-cutting nature of this work, the GRP Team will operate as an open team, actively soliciting input from Center staff (1) to facilitate Center-wide engagement on certain strategy, policy and budget matters, and (2) to facilitate the Center's country backstopping.

Governance and Rule of Law (GOV/ROL) Team
The newly combined GROL Team supports activities to improve the accountability, transparency and responsiveness of governing institutions, systems and processes. It also promotes legal and regulatory frameworks that improve order and security, legitimacy, checks and balances, and equal application and enforcement of the law. To this end, the GROL team's focus will not only be on work with governments but also on promoting citizen participation and engagement in governance and rule of law activities to build confidence and assure rights, privileges and obligations are equally accessible and fairly applied to all. The GROL Team will continue to cover the traditional governance and ROL subsectors. For governance, these include Legislative Strengthening,

Decentralization and Local Governance, Anticorruption, Security Sector Reform, Policy Reform, and Public Administration. Areas of focus for ROL include legal frameworks, building human and institutional capacity within the justice sector, strengthening linkages between police, prosecutors and courts, creating constituencies for legal reform, and increasing access to justice, including through the use of customary justice systems.

Human Rights (HR) Team

The HR Team provides field support and technical leadership on human-rights issues to USAID senior staff, operating units, and other USG agencies. The team identifies and disseminates best practices in the protection and promotion of physical integrity (such as freedom from torture, arrest and slavery) and other civil and political rights, and in the equal protection under the law (including protection for minorities and marginalized or vulnerable groups such as the lesbian, gay, bi-sexual and trans-gender [LGBT] community). The HR Team supports USAID Missions and DRG officers through training and technical support, including strategy and program design, assessments, and evaluations, and the provision of program funding and technical assistance. The empowerment of women, countering trafficking in persons, and implementing the Presidential Study Directive on preventing mass atrocities and genocide—these are the team's areas of special focus. The team also works to ensure that respect for human-rights principles is integrated throughout USG development cadre work.

Learning (L) Team

The Learning Team oversees cutting-edge impact evaluations, conducts research and innovations in the DRG sector, maintains strong relations with the international academic community, manages the DRG Knowledge Nexus (an interrelated set of DRG communities of practice) across the agency's DRG membership, and provides methodological support to the Center's other teams. In the short term, the purpose of the Learning Team is to manage knowledge and provide guidance regarding the most effective methods and programs for maximizing DRG impact with limited resources. In the medium term, the Learning Team's outcomes—which revolve around the creation, acquisition, dissemination and maintenance of knowledge—will enable USAID to reliably, efficiently and effectively improve democracy, human rights and governance in USAID recipient countries. In the long term, the Learning Team will enable the Center to influence agency and USG DRG policy through state-of-the-art knowledge of relevant social-science concepts and theories, rigorous analyses of empirical DRG program results, and advocacy in appropriate forums.

Strategic Planning (SP) Team

The Strategic Planning Team is a hybrid team that provides diverse support to all Center teams. The SP Team manages the Center's strategic planning, budget formulation and execution, and program implementation to support the Center's evidence-based technical leadership to Missions and the wider development community. The SP Team provides leadership to the Center in the areas of financial management, administration, and human resources; provides DRG training to development officers; and coordinates the Center's communication strategy in line with the goals of the Center and the DCHA Bureau, including (with the collaboration of the Learning Team) a DRG "community of practice" for DRG officers. The SP Team will take the lead for the Center in coordinating with the PPL Bureau on issues related to the agency's DRG Policy Task Team.

Gender Working Group (GWG)

The mission of the Gender Working Group (GWG) is to enable the DRG Center and DRG Officers in the field to promote and protect the human rights of women and girls, facilitate women's equal and meaningful participation in civic and political life, and better identify and address gender differences and inequalities as they relate to USAID's DRG work.

Training and Learning Team (TLT)

The goal of the Training Leadership Team (TLT) is to support the development and delivery of quality and relevant training to the Democracy, Human Rights and Governance (DRG) cadre, other USAID personnel and USG interagency partners and others deemed appropriate by the DRG Center. This includes developing training agendas, programs, identifying speakers and moderators, organizing content and delivering training and moderating programs. The TLT members are the link between teams, training participants, and other presenters, and must be fully engaged with their teams in the design and delivery of the training programs. The TLT will be chaired by the DRG Training Coordinator who will be responsible for providing the overarching training agenda and philosophical approach to training.

DRG CENTER STAFF DIRECTORY

NAME	TECHNICAL DIVISION	PHONE (202)	EMAIL ADDRESS
Dobberstein, Scott	Director, Acting	712-0487	sdobberstein@usaid.gov
Lott, Catie	Deputy Director	712-0385	clott@usaid.gov
Abbarno, Aaron	Learning	216-3756	aabbarno@usaid.gov
Akumu, Achieng	Governance & Rule of Law	712-0304	aakumu@usaid.gov
Athreya, Bama	Civil Society & Media	216-3808	bathreya@usaid.gov
Ayer, Victoria	Governance & Rule of Law	712-1857	vayer@usaid.gov
Barden, Kenneth	Governance & Rule of Law	712-0527	kbarden@usaid.gov
Benton Cooney, Jessica	Strategic Planning	712-1102	jbentoncooney@usaid.gov
Billera, Mark	Global & Regional Policy	712-5139	mbillera@usaid.gov
Black, David	Global & Regional Policy	712-0599	dblack@usaid.gov
Bonoff, Nicole	Learning	712-0851	nbonoff@usaid.gov
Bradow, Michael	Global & Regional Policy	216-3488	mbradow@usaid.gov
Browning, Julie	Global & Regional Policy	712-5743	jbrowning@usaid.gov
Buckley, Colin	Governance & Rule of Law	712-4293	cbuckley@usaid.gov
Bushey, Adam	Governance & Rule of Law	712-4285	abushey@usaid.gov
Chilton, Rachel	Strategic Planning	712-0590	rchilton@usaid.gov
Colby, Marina	Human Rights	216-3547	macolby@usaid.gov
Crawford, Keith	Governance & Rule of Law	712-1471	kcrawford@usaid.gov
Daniels, Phyllis	Strategic Planning	712-0479	pdaniels@usaid.gov
del Castillo, Christina	Cross-Sectoral Programs	712-4508	cdelcastillo@usaid.gov
Demers, Chris	Cross-Sectoral Programs	712-0083	cdemers@usaid.gov
Denham, Julie	Governance & Rule of Law	712-5845	jdenham@usaid.gov
Ehmann, Claire	Civil Society & Media	712-0751	cehmann@usaid.gov
Eitel, Sue	Human Rights	789-1500	seitel@usaid.gov
Garrett, Ben	Cross-Sectoral Programs	216-3084	bgarrett@usaid.gov
Glover, Robert	Global & Regional Policy	712-4948	rglover@usaid.gov
Goldenbaum, Mark	Human Rights	712-0729	mgoldenbaum@usaid.gov
Greenberg, Natasha	Human Rights	712-4722	ngreenberg@usaid.gov
Hanley, Brian	Global & Regional Policy	712-1806	bhanley@usaid.gov
Harvey, Stephanie	Strategic Planning	712-0973	sharvey@usaid.gov
Hayes, Martin	Human Rights	789-1500	mhayes@usaid.gov
Haynes, Joshua	Civil Society & Media	712-0836	johaynes@usaid.gov
Holmes, Morgan	Learning	712-0175	moholmes@usaid.gov
Horvath, Rob	Human Rights	789-1500	rhorvath@usaid.gov
Hovetter, Valerie	Strategic Planning	712-0189	vhovetter@usaid.gov
Hunter, Patricia	Civil Society & Media	216-3534	phunter@usaid.gov
Ilirjani, Altin	Learning	712-5783	ailirjani@usaid.gov
Ivantcheva, Assia	Elections & Political Transitions	712-0288	aivantcheva@usaid.gov
Jacobstein, David	Cross-Sectoral Programs	712-1469	djacobstein@usaid.gov
Jenkins, Sandy	Human Rights	789-1500	sjenkins@usaid.gov
Joshi, Ajit	Cross-Sectoral Programs	712-5374	ajoshi@usaid.gov
Keane, Brian	Human Rights	712-0712	bkeane@usaid.gov

Keshishian, Mike	Governance & Rule of Law	712-4725	mkeshishian@usaid.gov
Koenig, Mark	Civil Society & Media	712-1507	mkoenig@usaid.gov
Koumbairia-Thomas, Edith	Strategic Planning	712-4117	ekoumbairiathomas@usaid.gov
Lam, Vy	Cross-Sectoral Programs	712-5708	vlam@usaid.gov
Leavitt, Virginia	Strategic Planning	712-0965	vleavitt@usaid.gov
Lopez, Summer	Global & Regional Policy	712-4183	slopez@usaid.gov
Maxson, Leah	Human Rights	789-1500	lmaxson@usaid.gov
McEnery, Tess	Elections & Political Transitions	712-0658	tmcenery@usaid.gov
McGovern, Patrick	Global & Regional Policy	712-5584	pmcgovern@usaid.gov
McGregor-Mirghani, Lisa	Cross-Sectoral Programs	712-4632	lmcgregor-mirghani@usaid.gov
Michels, Andy	Governance & Rule of Law	712-0777	amichels@usaid.gov
Miller, Kendra	Strategic Planning	712-5576	kemiller@usaid.gov
Mishler, William	Learning	712-0778	wmishler@usaid.gov
Mitchell, Carrie	Global & Regional Policy	712-1537	camitchell@usaid.gov
Molina, Stephanie	Global & Regional Policy	712-5346	smolina@usaid.gov
Moore, Monica	Elections & Political Transitions	216-3276	momoore@usaid.gov
Moss, Jill	Civil Society & Media	712-0477	jmoss@iie.org
Pavlovic, Laura	Cross-Sectoral Programs	712-0962	lpavlovic@usaid.gov
Poore, Kristin	Human Rights	216-3388	kpoore@usaid.gov
Rasool, Heela	Cross-Sectoral Programs	216-3366	hrasool@usaid.gov
Rogers, Sharon	Strategic Planning	712-4918	shrogers@usaid.gov
Rothblum, Corrine	Cross-Sectoral Programs	712-0079	crothblum@usaid.gov
Sahley, Carol	Elections & Political Transitions	712-0608	csahley@usaid.gov
Savino, Cathy	Human Rights	789-1500	csavino@usaid.gov
Schulz, Keith	Governance & Rule of Law	712-4219	keschulz@usaid.gov
Seyfried, Lauren	Strategic Planning	216-3752	lseyfried@usaid.gov
Solomon, Andrew	Human Rights	712-1351	asolomon@iie.org
Sturr, Kevin	Human Rights	712-5725	ksturr@usaid.gov
Swift, Sarah	Cross-Sectoral Programs	712-4777	sswift@usaid.gov
Taggart, Joe	Strategic Planning	712-0172	jtaggart@usaid.gov
Vanness, Jeff	Elections & Political Transitions	712-4516	jvanness@usaid.gov
Werbel, Julie	Governance & Rule of Law	712-1711	jwerbel@usaid.gov
Werth, Sara	Governance & Rule of Law	712-1946	swerth@usaid.gov
White, Christopher	Strategic Planning	216-3194	chrwhite@usaid.gov
Widdersheim, Nicole	Human Rights	712-5325	nwiddersheim@usaid.gov
Williams, Lisa	Cross-Sectoral Programs	216-3434	liwilliams@usaid.gov
Williamson, John	Human Rights	804-232-3408	jwilliamson@usaid.gov
Woocher, Lawrence	Human Rights	326-7673	lwoocher@usaid.gov
Yerkes, Maryanne	Civil Society & Media	712-0915	myerkes@usaid.gov
Zeitlin, Veronica	Human Rights	712-4585	vzeitlin@usaid.gov

BIOGRAPHIES OF DRG OFFICE STAFF

Director

Scott Dobberstein is the **Acting Director** of the DRG Center. Prior to joining the Center, Scott served as Deputy Director of the USAID Mission in Indonesia. Prior to serving in Indonesia, Scott served as a DRG Team Leader in Uganda and Senegal. He also worked on DRG programs for the E&E Bureau and the USAID Mission in Poland. Before working on DRG programs, Scott served at USAID's Regional Housing and Urban Development Office for the Near East and North Africa in Tunis. Scott started his career with USAID as a Presidential Management Intern (Presidential Management Fellow) in USAID's Office of Housing and Urban Programs. He earned a Master's Degree in Arab Studies and International Relations from Georgetown University and a Bachelor's Degree in History from St. Olaf College. He was a Fulbright Scholar in Damascus, Syria.

Deputy Director

Catie Lott is the **Deputy Director** for the **DRG Center**. For the past dozen years she has worked as a Democracy, Human Rights, and Governance Officer with postings in Africa, Asia, and Latin America. She has managed a wide spectrum of programs that cross all DRG areas of expertise, and been a strong proponent of early DRG integration attempts. Prior to joining USAID, she worked as a journalist for a variety of publications in the United States and Africa covering human interest stories, travel, and politics. Catie has a BA from the University of California Santa Barbara, an MA from Syracuse University, and is currently working on her PhD focused on women's political leadership.

L. Achieng Akumu currently serves as the **Senior Rule of Law Advisor** with the **Governance and Rule of Law Team.** She assists the Team in the development and implementation of research, monitoring, and evaluation of RoL activities; conducts assessments and evaluations of Mission's RoL activities; develops strategies, designs programs and performance monitoring plans for RoL activities; strengthens liaisons between USAID with relevant U.S. government agencies, donors and implementers; and designs training programs for Foreign Service officers and other staff on rule of law topics including informal justice systems. Achieng's geographical expertise includes Africa, Southern Asia and limited experience in the Colombia and Jamaica. She speaks French and Swahili. Previously, Achieng worked for National Democratic Institute as Chief of Party of a Legislative Strengthening Program in Namibia and as a regional program officer in southern Africa. She has also worked as legislative attorney for the New York State Assembly on South African issues, and as Legislative Director for 2 Members of Congress from the U.S. House of Representatives. Achieng has also consulted for UNDP, CEDPA and the World Health Organization/Africa on legal reform and health initiatives. Achieng holds a B.A. from Russell Sage College, a diploma from Universite de Besancon (France) and a J.D. from Syracuse University College of Law.

Bama Athreya is a **Senior Specialist, Labor and Employment Rights**. She has twenty years' experience on international labor rights issues, and has previously worked for the AFL-CIO Solidarity Center, International Labor Rights Forum, and International Labour Organization. She has developed and led multi-country projects in Latin America, sub-Saharan Africa and Asia on the rights of working women, on labor law implementation, on forced and child labor, and on ethical business practices. She has developed and led multi-stakeholder initiatives with global corporations on labor compliance, and has worked and written extensively on labor rights in US trade policy. She served as one of the founding Board members of the Sweatfree Purchasing Consortium, an entity serving state and city governments in the United States who have adopted legislative or executive commitments to ethical procurement. In 2009 she was appointed by Secretary of Agriculture Tom Vilsack to a special Consultative Group on Forced and Child Labor. She speaks French, Spanish, Chinese and Indonesian.

Victoria Ayer a **Senior Anti-corruption and Good Governance Advisor** with the **Governance and Rule of Law Team.** With more than a decade of experience advising and assisting civil society and political leaders in the Middle East, Southeast Asia, the Balkans and Africa in an effort to expand dialogue, ensure accountability and strengthen democratic practices, before joining USAID, Victoria served as a human rights lawyer for the United Nations with a focus on drafting and negotiating multilateral agreements. She has served as the Chief of Party for a multi-pronged anti-corruption project in Cambodia that included: successful passage of anti-corruption law; investigative journalism training; capacity building for an anti-corruption commission; and support for a locally-led petition effort that garnered signatures of 1 million+ citizens. She is a former US Congressional staffer with a wealth of practical experience in formal and informal politics. In the DRG Center, she backstops Ghana and serves as the focal point for Making All Voices Count: A Grand Challenge for Development, the Extractive Industry Transparency Initiative and the Open Government Partnership. She earned her B.A. in Political Science from Rice University and her law degree from Boston University School of Law.

Kenneth Barden is **a Senior Governance and Anticorruption Officer** for DRG. For several years, Ken was an independent consultant for several international development projects, including ones funded by USAID, the MCC, World Bank, UN, Asian Development Bank and others. Ken served as Team Leader for the USAID-administered MCC Threshold Indonesia Control of Corruption Project in Indonesia, working on anticorruption and judicial reform. Immediately prior to joining USAID, Ken was an advisor with the USAID Modernizing Financial Institutions project in the West Bank, where he led implementation of anti-money laundering and anticorruption activities. Ken's experience includes work in Eastern Europe, Central and Southeastern Asia, Oceania, the Middle East and Africa. He also has over 15 years of experience in municipal government. Ken holds a Juris Doctor from Indiana University, and a Bachelor's degree in Political Science from University of Indianapolis, as well as post-graduate work in Disaster Management from the University of Wisconsin and in International Humanitarian Law from the National Academy of Legal Studies and Research (NALSAR), in Hyderabad, India. He has written extensively on financial integrity and risk management issues and is a Certified Anti Money Laundering Specialist (CAMS), as well as a Certified Financial Crime Specialist (CFCS).

Jessica Benton Cooney is the **Communications Specialist** on the **Strategic Planning Team**. She serves as the strategic communication advisor for the outreach efforts of the DRG Center. This includes external/internal communications, product development, and multi-media (video, photography). Prior, she was in Liberia on the DAI Feed the Future (Food and Enterprise Development) project, and the Education Development Center (EDC) Advancing Youth project, both funded by USAID, as well as the United Nations Population Fund. Jessica was a communications officer for Pact in Washington, D.C., and served as the web data manager for the USAID/Afghanistan website, while also backstopping the Department of Communication (DOC) at the USAID mission in Kabul, Afghanistan. Jessica also covered elections, politics, and the House as a staff writer and production editor for The Congressional Quarterly in Washington, D.C. She has her master's degree in Human Rights from the London School of Economics and Political Science. She was also a Peace Corps volunteer in El Salvador.

Mark Billera serves as a **Democracy Specialist** and is the **Regional Coordinator for Africa** on the **Global & Regional Policy Team**. He previously worked and conducted research in Cameroon. Mark has an A.B. in political science and economics from Duke University. He has an M.A. and is finishing his Ph.D. in political science from the University of California, Los Angeles.

David Black is the **Team Leader for the Global & Regional Policy Team**. He has served overseas as the Democracy Office Director for USAID/Kosovo, and as the Senior Democracy Advisor for Ukraine, Belarus and Moldova with USAID/Kyiv. He began his USAID career in 1994 in the E&E Bureau's Office of Democracy and Governance, and his previous work in DCHA/DRG includes a stint on the Civil Society & Media Team, serving as the Regional Coordinator for Europe & Eurasia, and leading an early initiative to improve evaluations of DRG assistance programs. He speaks Russian and has lived and studied extensively in the Europe and Eurasia region. He holds a B.A. from Colgate University and an M.A. in International Relations from the Maxwell School at Syracuse University.

Mike Bradow is the **Asia Regional Coordinator** within the DRG Center's **Global & Regional Policy Team**. In this capacity, he serves as a liaison to field missions, USAID/W regional and functional offices, the interagency and other external stakeholders on DRG policy priorities and programming in Asia. After joining USAID as a Foreign Service Officer in 2010, Mike worked in the Democracy & Governance Office in the USAID/Central Asian Republics regional mission and focused on local governance programming in Tajikistan, regional civil society and media initiatives and DRG evaluations. His previous work includes managing civil society, human rights and new media projects in both Latin America and the Caucasus for Freedom House, and also as a consultant to other USAID, State/DRL and OTI implementing partners. Mike received his BA in Political Science from Wake Forest University and a Masters in Public Policy from the University of Chicago.

Julie Browning serves as the **Senior Democracy and Governance Advisor for Afghanistan and Pakistan,** as a member of the **Global & Regional Policy Team**. Prior, she served as a Democracy Advisor for USAID's Afghanistan Democracy and Governance Office and as the Senior Democracy and Governance Advisor for the Middle East/Iraq Office. Julie provides strategic direction and technical guidance on democracy and governance programming broadly with a focus on electoral institutions and political representation at national and local levels. Beyond this she coordinates the bureau's technical inputs to these countries and plays a leading role in a number of related inter-agency fora. She has spent the past ten years as a consultant advising or managing human rights/refugee and governance programs for the UN High Commissioner for Refugees, The Asia Foundation, the Office of the High Representative, Associates in Rural Development and the American Refugee Committee within Jordan, Afghanistan and throughout the Balkans. Julie holds a Masters Degree in International Studies with an emphasis on International Politics and Human Rights from the University of Denver.

CPT Adam Bushey is a **Governance and Rule of Law expert** on the **Governance and Rule of Law Team**. CPT Bushey has worked on issues related to counter-insurgency, civilian-military operations, Rule of Law, and governance worldwide. At USAID, prior to joining the DRG Center, he has been assigned to the Performance Division of M/MPBP, the Office of General Council, and the Afghanistan-Pakistan Task Force. CPT Bushey also currently serves as a reserve JAG Officer in the Army. He coordinated the 86th Infantry Brigade's Rule of Law (ROL) and governance efforts in four provinces in RC-East, Afghanistan. He was awarded the U.S. Bronze Star Medal for meritorious service. CPT Bushey attained his undergraduate degree from Le Moyne College where he graduated Magna Cum Laude with a double major in political science and economics. Before and during law school, where he graduated with Honors, Mr. Bushey worked for the New York State Assembly.

Christina del Castillo currently serves as a **Governance Advisor** with the **Cross-Sectoral Programs Team.** Christina's areas of specialization include public sector governance, citizen participation and aid effectiveness. She provides technical guidance to USAID offices worldwide to incorporate good governance practices to strengthen host country systems, increase transparency and accountability, and decrease corruption. Previously, Christina served as DRG's Anticorruption Advisor, and before that she served in the Latin America and Caribbean Bureau, Office for Central America and Mexico. Prior to joining USAID she was a Presidential Management Fellow in the International Affairs Office of the National Oceanic and Atmospheric Administration. Christina served as a Peace Corps Volunteer in Guatemala where she provided technical assistance to local government and conduct research regarding democratic participation in a post-conflict environment. She has a B.A. in Political Science from California State University, San Marcos and an M.P.A. in International Development from Rutgers University.

Rachel Chilton is a **Program Support Specialist** for the Center's **Strategic Planning Team**. Rachel assists the communications specialist with the execution of internal and external communications tasks including outreach strategies, planning events, social media, website maintenance, and product development. She also on-boards new staff to the Center, is the office liaison between AMS/HR/SEC for Center staff, and backstops official correspondence and travel. Before joining USAID, she completed a communications internship with the Carnegie Endowment for International Peace. Prior to that, she spent a year in Kaohsiung, Taiwan, working as an English teacher for the Fulbright Program. Rachel received a B.A. in International Relations & Global Affairs with a concentration in Mandarin Chinese from Eckerd College. She studied in Shanghai and Xiamen, China as well as in Amsterdam, The Netherlands during two semesters abroad. Rachel also had the opportunity to further her Mandarin language skills by attending the Chinese Language School at Middlebury College. Rachel volunteered at the Florida Center for Survivors of Torture during her last year in college and continues to be interested in human rights abuses.

Keith Crawford is a **Democracy Specialist** for the **Governance and Rule of Law Division.** He oversees the Rights Consortium Cooperative Agreement (Freedom House, ABA, and NDI), which supports rule of law and human rights activities, as well as oversees the Rule of law Indefinite Quantity Contract. With expertise in the Europe and Eurasia region and language competency in Finnish, Keith provides field support and technical assistance to USAID Missions worldwide; serves as a rule of law trainer to Democracy and Governance Officers and others; and assists the rule of law division with the development of technical leadership publications and best practices. He has participated in numerous democracy and governance and rule of law workshops sponsored by USAID, the World Bank, and think tanks like the Carnegie Endowment. Prior to joining USAID he served as an Assistant District Attorney in the Office of the District Attorney, Brooklyn, N.Y., and worked in a private law practice in Norfolk, Virginia. Keith holds a B.A. from Old Dominion University and a J.D. from Howard University School of Law.

Phyllis Daniels currently works on the **Strategic Planning Team** as the **Financial Management Specialist.** Prior to this she worked as a Human Resources Assistant with the Human Resources Civil Service Personnel Division, Recruitment and Staffing Branch. Phyllis also served in the United States Army as a Financial and Personnel Specialist and was honorably discharged. She continued her civilian career in Human Resources Management. Phyllis has worked for the National Endowment for the Humanities, Peace Corps, and the Department of Commerce. She pursued her education at Northern Virginia Community College.

Chris Demers works on the **Cross-Sectoral Programs Team** within the Center for Democracy, Rights and Governance, which addresses Implementation and Procurement Reform and DRG Integration for the Center. Chris is familiar with the Public Financial Management Risk Assessment Framework, DRG considerations in that process, models for G2G assistance, and capacity building in PFM and Public Accountability. Chris also works closely with other offices in DCHA on resiliency through better governance. Before joining the Center, Chris worked in the Afghanistan mission on public administration reform and local governance. Prior to USAID, Chris worked in the NGO community, including the International Bar Association, Norwegian Refugee Council and International Rescue Committee on governance, rule of law and human rights programming. Chris holds a JD from the City University of New York and a BA from Georgetown University.

Julie Denham is a **Senior Advisor** for the **Elections and Political Transitions Team** and assists USAID Missions to design and implement innovative and effective elections and political party programs. She previously served as the Team Lead for Governance, Rule of Law and Security for USAID's Haiti Task Team. Prior to joining USAID, Julie worked for 12 years with the National Democratic Institute (NDI), serving as a Washington, DC-based Senior Program Manager for elections and legislative strengthening programs in Nigeria, Sierra Leone and Guinea, and as Resident Director for NDI's Algeria office. Julie earned her Bachelor's degree in Government and

International Relations from Smith College, and a Master of Science in Foreign Service degree from Georgetown University. She is fluent in French and has basic Arabic and Spanish language skills.

Claire Ehmann is the **Civil Society and Media Team leader.** She has focused on democracy, peace, and security issues in the Middle East and Asia, and also served as a Senior Civil Society Advisor in USAID's Europe and Eurasia bureau, Formerly, she was editor-in-chief of the NGO Sustainability Index, USAID's chief civil society analytical measurement tool. Claire is an expert on NGO legal environments, NGO sustainability issues, and working with civil society in authoritarian environments. She also has technical expertise designing endowments. Prior to joining USAID, Claire served as the Balkans human rights specialist for the Department of State's Bureau for Democracy, Human Rights, and Labor and worked on NGO capacity building in Eastern Europe and the Balkans for Freedom House and Partners for Democratic Change. Claire was a Fulbright Scholar in Burkina Faso, studying African cinema. Claire has a Masters in International Public Affairs from the Woodrow Wilson School at Princeton University, where she specialized in partnerships between international and local NGOs. Her undergraduate degree is from the College of William and Mary.

Sue Eitel is a physical therapist and serves as the **Senior Rehabilitation Advisor** under the **Vulnerable Populations Program**. Her work focuses on supporting programs and activities under the Leahy War Victims Fund and Wheelchair Program. She has over 25 years of international experience working in/with physical rehabilitation programs in less resourced settings.

Bob Glover is a **Democracy Officer** on the **Global & Regional Policy Team.** Previously, Bob served as the Bamyan Provincial Reconstruction Team (PRT) lead in Afghanistan, covering the full range of Governance and Development programs and working with Afghan counterparts at provincial, municipal and district government as well as with Afghan civil society, implementing partners and national line ministers. Bob's previous work experience includes 10 years leading an NGO in conflict resolution and community development, 3 years in Higher Education successfully promoting public – private partnerships, and 10 years in agribusiness developing markets and value chains across Asia. Bob and his wife served as Peace Corps volunteers in the Moroccan Sahara where they worked with associations, cooperatives, municipal and regional government to promote opportunities for women in small business development and civil society. Bob, a Retired Colonel, Army Civil Affairs, is a graduate of the US Military Academy, West Point, and has an MBA from Tulane University. In Washington, Bob provides technical and strategy support to USAID missions in the Middle East and North Africa (MENA) advancing DRG policies and programs across the region – especially those like Libya undergoing significant political transition. Bob is conversational in Arabic and French.

Mark Goldenbaum leads the **Human Rights Team's** work in **Atrocity Prevention**. He is provides support to implement the Presidential Directive on Atrocity Prevention and also helped launch the Atrocity Prevention Tech Challenge. Prior to USAID, Mark most recently served with Internews Network as Program Director for the Central Asia and South Caucuses regions, where he oversaw media development initiatives and other DRG programs. He has also worked with Mercy Corps, both as Country Representative in Uzbekistan and as Program Director for the USAID-funded Peaceful Communities Initiative, a community mobilization and conflict mitigation program in the Ferghana Valley of Kyrgyzstan, Tajikistan, and Uzbekistan. Mark was a Peace Corps Volunteer in Kazakhstan. He holds a Master's of Arts in International Relations from the Fletcher School of Law and Diplomacy at Tufts University and a Bachelor's degree in English from the University of Texas, Austin.

Natasha Greenberg is a **Human Rights Program Specialist** in the DCHA/DRG Center of Excellence. She is a member of the **Human Rights Team**, with a primary focus on counter-trafficking in persons. She also works on issues related to transitional justice and is co-chair of the DRG Gender Working group. Natasha previously worked in the Office of Women in Development, providing technical assistance to the DCHA bureau on issues related to gender and conflict and governance. She has completed rotations in USAID South Africa and in the State Department and served as a Civilian Response Corps Stabilization Team member in South Sudan, reporting on security concerns and working to enhance stability in three states in South Sudan. Prior to her work at USAID, Natasha was Assistant Director at Facing History and Ourselves, an NGO focused on education to prevent genocide and promote reconciliation in countries such as Rwanda, Colombia, Bosnia and South Africa. She also worked on conflict resolution and development issues with local NGOs in Uganda and Ecuador, and on the Israeli-Palestinian Negotiation Project and the development of case studies through Mercy Corps and the Harvard Program on Negotiation. Natasha is a trained community mediator who has mediated disputes in San Francisco and Boston. She received a Bachelor of Science from Cornell University and a Master's degree from the Johns Hopkins School of Advanced International Studies (SAIS).

Brian D. Hanley is a **Senior Democracy and Governance Field Advisor** serving on the **Global and Regional Policy (GRP) team**. He delivers surge, technical, and strategy/policy backstopping support to crisis and stabilization countries, and leads DRG Center efforts in provision of democratic development assistance to Syria. Prior to joining USAID, he served as Asia Director for Search for Common Ground (SFCG), where he led DRG and peacebuilding programs in Indonesia, Nepal, Pakistan, Sri Lanka, and Timor-Leste. He also oversaw SFCG's work in Indonesia, as Country Director. Before that, he was Chief of Party (COP) on a NGO Sector Strengthening Program in Timor-Leste, implemented by ACDI/VOCA and Columbia University's Center for International Conflict Resolution (CICR). He was a U.S. Peace Corps Volunteer in Kingston, Jamaica, and has served at various times in the U.S. Congress, under two Democratic Senators: Dodd (104th) and Wellstone (109th). Brian earned his Bachelor's degree in Political Science and Sociology from the University of Connecticut, and a Master's of International Affairs from Columbia University's School of International and Public Affairs (SIPA). He is fluent in Tetum, and has intermediate Bahasa Indonesia, Jamaican Patois, and Spanish language skills.

Stephanie Harvey currently works as a **Management/Program Analyst** on the **Strategic Planning Team**. She studied Business Administration at Strayer University. Twenty three of her twenty nine year federal government experience has been spent with USAID. Prior to her time here, she joined the E3 Bureau in 2004 where she served as the Program Operations Assistant in the former WID office. In 2007, she served as the Program Analyst and has experience in budget planning and information systems, including Phoenix, GLAAS, and FACTS Info.

Martin Hayes is a **Senior Technical Advisor for the Displaced Children and Orphans Fund (DCOF)**. DCOF is in the Vulnerable Populations portfolio, managed by Rob Horvath, which is housed within the Human Rights Team. DCOF's goal is to improve the safety, wellbeing, and development of vulnerable children, with particular attention to preserving and supporting appropriate family care. Martin's work includes supporting the development of new projects, providing technical support to implementing partners and developing and sharing technical resources with Agency and interagency partners.

Joshua Haynes is a **Senior Development Technologist and Media Adviser** on the **Civil Society and Media Team** where he focuses on the nexus of technology, media, civil society, Internet freedom, information security and democracy, rights and governance. Previously, he was involved in the private sector, working in analytics and technology consulting across Europe, as well as on international development-focused ICT projects in Sub-Saharan and North Africa, Central America, the Caribbean and South Asia, in the areas of media, new media, civil society, stability, democracy, apps, the mobile gender gap and financial inclusion. Joshua received degrees from Boston University and The Fletcher School at Tufts University and speaks a number of languages including Arabic (Modern Standard and Maghrebi), French, German and Spanish.

Morgan Holmes is an **Evaluation Specialist** with DRG's **Learning Team**. Ms. Holmes was recently a Program Manager on OTI's Afghanistan and Pakistan teams where she managed Stabilization contracts and agreements as well as designing and procuring evaluations of OTI programs in those countries. Prior to joining USAID, she worked at the World Bank's Independent Evaluation Group and as an M&E consultant in the private sector, designing and conducting performance and impact evaluations of USAID, State, World Bank and DfID programs. Ms. Holmes also assisted in the start-up of the International Initiative for Impact Evaluation (3ie). Before specializing in M&E, Ms. Holmes worked for NDI and IRI implementing political party, civil society, and media strengthening programs. Morgan helped establish IRI's Iraq program, where she focused on civil society capacity building. She has managed programs in Afghanistan, the Czech Republic, the DRC, Indonesia, Iraq, Kenya, Pakistan, Peru, the Philippines, Slovakia, and Venezuela. She holds a BSc from Georgetown University's School of Foreign Service, an MSc from the London School of Economics.

Rob Horvath is the **Fund manager** for the **Vulnerable Populations** portfolio housed within the **Human Rights Team**. As a member of USAID's disability team, he was the lead drafter of the recently adopted policy directives on inclusive development practices and procedures. He provides program design, management, and monitoring and evaluation support for the various Vulnerable Populations' funds. Previously, he oversaw regional grants programs in USAID's Regional Development Mission in Asia. Prior to joining USAID, Rob served as both a volunteer and director of pre-service training for Peace Corps/Thailand as well as with the office of vocational rehabilitation for the State of Michigan, Department of Education. His geographic expertise is S.E. Asia. He holds an M.A. in counseling psychology and a B.S. in Human Resource Development and is a certified trainer with both the Virginia State and National Parent/Teacher Associations.

Valerie Hovetter specializes in **Project Design and Monitoring and Evaluation (M&E)/Reporting** as part of the **Strategic Planning Team**. She is also a member of the **DRG Gender Working Group**. She has managed numerous complex, multi-million dollar USAID and other donor-funded international development projects, developed technical strategies, led project work-planning workshops, and has conducted assessments in anti-corruption, civil society strengthening, as well as other sectors such as agriculture, food security, health, and finance. Valerie has also provided specialized support in monitoring and evaluation, as the M&E Advisor for Sub-Saharan Africa and Haiti at Chemonics International. She is fluent in French and has 12 years of experience focused on Sub-Saharan Africa, with direct experience in more than 10 African countries. She co-backstops Haiti for the DRG Center. Valerie was a Peace Corps volunteer in Togo. She earned her B.A. in Anthropology from University of Arizona and her M.P.A in International Development Administration from Rutgers University.

Altin Ilirjani serves as the **Team Leader** on the **Learning Team**. He assists the DRG Office in implementing the National Academy of Sciences recommendations for improving democracy assistance through impact evaluations and research, and provides technical expertise on improving standards, methods and use of democracy and governance surveys. Previously, Altin worked for the World Bank Group in Washington DC, the Open Society Institute in Budapest, and taught courses in comparative politics and East Central Europe politics at the University of North Carolina, Chapel Hill. He has served as a visiting scholar at Duke University, 2001-2002; the International Monetary Fund, 2000-2001; the European University Institute in Florence, 1999-2000; and at the London School of Economics, 2000. Altin served as the principal investigator of the 2005 and 2009 Albanian National Election Study, part of the Comparative Study of Electoral Systems of the University of Michigan, and has conducted extensive field research in Cyprus, Turkey, Kosovo, Macedonia, Hungary, and Albania. Altin has a Ph.D. with majors in comparative politics and public policy.

Assia Ivantcheva, as the **Senior Adviser** with the **Elections and Political Transitions Team**, provides assistance to missions globally. Her primary geographic focuses are countries in the Europe and Eurasia, Central and Southeast Asia regions. Functional areas of expertise include international election standards and election monitoring, voter education, election management bodies, political party and parliamentary development. Until 2009 she was a career foreign service officer, serving as the Director of the Democracy Office in Serbia and the Deputy Director of the Democracy Office at the Regional Mission in Kyiv, managing democracy programs in Ukraine, Belarus, and Moldova. Assia was the Deputy and Acting Head of the Human Rights Department at OSCE's Office for Democratic Institutions and Human Rights (ODIHR) for three tears. She holds a Ph. D. in International Relations from the School of International Service at American University, a B.A. from Dartmouth College and a M.A. equivalent degree in Arabic Studies from Sofia University.

David Jacobstein serves as a **Democracy Specialist** in the **Cross-Sectoral Programs Team** of the Center of Excellence on Democracy, Human Rights, and Governance, where he focuses on issues of local capacity development. Previously, he worked for Pact, a leading global capacity development organization, in a number of positions, most recently as Senior Program Manager for Governance. He contributed to the design and implementation of programs focusing on civil society advocacy, network analysis and strengthening, organizational development, decentralization, and community engagement in countries including Kenya, Nigeria, Ukraine, Tajikistan, and Malawi. He also conducted research into capacity areas of networks and using social network mapping to contribute to network strengthening, and developed training materials to assist Pact in introducing core DG concepts to its other program portfolios. He previously served Pact as Senior Program Manager for their Global Civil Society Strengthening LWA, managing a portfolio of awards to US and international partners of over $100 million in over 25 countries. In 2010, he was based in Mongolia to manage a community-engaged health program focused on communities near large mining operations. Prior to working with Pact, he worked on rule of law and access to justice issues for the American Bar Association in Eastern Europe and Asia.

Sandra Jenkins serves as the **Point of Contact** for the **Vulnerable Populations Program** activities conducted under Global Health's Leadership, Management and Governance and Accelovate projects. She also serves as **Communications Specialist** for the Vulnerable Populations Programs. In the latter role, she functions as editor, publications coordinator, and web-content provider. She previously worked in the Office of Health and as editor for the POPTECH contract, Office of Population. Sandra holds a B.A. in Theatrical Design from the University of Virginia. She has extensive experience in editing and design for publication and the web, and has earned professional certificates in Editing and Publications Management from The George Washington University's College of Professional Studies. She expects to receive an M.A. in the History of Decorative Arts in December 2008 through her combined studies at New York University, Parsons: The New School for Design, and the Corcoran College of Art and Design.

Ajit Joshi concurrently serves as **Democracy Specialist for Local Capacity Development** as well as the Agency's **Acting Senior LGBT Coordinator**, Policy and Program Advisor, for which he has earned USAID's Distinguished Honor Award. He has served as a Senior Program Officer in the Bureau for Democracy, Conflict, and Humanitarian Assistance, Special Assistant to the Counselor to the Agency, Team Leader in the Office of Private Voluntary Cooperation for a $22 million NGO capacity-building program particularly in conflict-affected areas, Supervisory Democracy Specialist in the Africa Bureau overseeing a $41 million communication, peace building, and governance program, and a conflict management specialist in the Africa Bureau, for which he earned USAID's Superior Honor Award. Mr. Joshi received a Bachelor of Arts in international relations from Tufts University, a Fulbright Fellowship to study in India, and a Master of international affairs from Columbia University's School of International and Public Affairs. He has expertise in gender, human rights, strategic planning, leadership development, training, coaching, facilitation, and staff care.

Mike Keshishian joined USAID in 1996. He is a **Local Government and Decentralization Advisor** and is jointly funded by DRG/G and EGAT Urban Programs. Mike lived in Armenia for five years where he worked on

World Bank and USAID-funded projects. Mike speaks fluent German and proficient Armenian. He has a Master's degree in Urban Planning.

Mark Koenig serves as a **Senior Media Advisor** on the **Civil Society and Media Team**. He focuses on strengthening *independent media*, assisting Missions or other operational units to design, procure, implement and evaluate programs that: build normative-legal-regulatory environments for freer media, raise the professional level of journalists, train media business managers, build the financial self-sustainability of media outlets, upgrade audience ratings and other industry data services, and/or strengthen media-sector CSOs. More broadly, his work involves DRG assessments, civil society support, plus cross-sector, integrated development communications, strengthening the media's roles to promote such diverse development objectives as: public health, education, agricultural extension, economic growth, elections coverage, conflict mitigation, etc. He has traveled on USAID business to well over two dozen countries in Eurasia, the Middle East, Latin America and Africa. Mark holds an MAIS from Johns Hopkins SAIS and a Ph.D. in Comparative Politics from Columbia University. He taught political science for five years at NYU, Northwestern University and the University of Maryland, College Park, offering courses on comparative politics, political culture, ethno-national politics, Chinese, Russian and Eurasian political development. He served a year as a Fulbright Scholar at the Moscow State University Journalism Department. With varying degrees of fluency, he speaks Russian, French and Italian.

Edith Koumbairia-Thomas supports the **Strategic Planning Team**. She volunteered for the American Red Cross, assisting in planning Network and Fundraising events. Edith did some consulting work with PATH, in the capacity of Program Support, translating technical documents in French. She co-backstopped the PEPFAR led-project by the HIV/TB team in Washington and the field Office in DRC. While at PATH, Edith utilized her creative, organizational, technical and interpersonal skills to assist in the planning of one of the largest "Stop TB Conference" held by the World Health Organization (WHO) in Washington DC. She holds a B.A and B.S in Economics and Finance from Central State University and an MBA in Water Resources from Albany State University. She is a native French speaker.

Vy Lam is a **AAAS Fellow** on the **Human Rights Team** who works on integrating **Lesbian, Gay, Bisexual and Transgender** (LGBT) concerns into USAID policies and programs. The work involves reforming operations, conducting field research, and developing data and analytics to support the advancement of the LGBT agenda in various development sectors. He is an interdisciplinary scientist with a background in microbiome physiology, radiopathology, viral immunology, cardiovascular diseases, and tissue engineering. Vy received his Ph.D. from University of Wisconsin, Madison where he studied the dynamics of vesicular stomatitis replication and its induction of immunity.

Virginia Leavitt is a **Senior Training Coordinator** on the **Strategic Planning Team**. She brings 14 years of overseas rule of law experience in the area of training, capacity building, and institution development. Most recently Virginia worked in partnership with the Supreme Court of Liberia to establish through the American Bar Association the national judicial training institute including a year-long curriculum for potential new magistrates. In Bulgaria she worked East West Management Institute for 7 years in the area of rule of law which included the establishment of the national judicial training center. During this tenure she organized 3 national conferences with over 1300 participants each. While in Egypt, Virginia assisted the Ministry of Justice in the revamping of the Egyptian judicial training center and introduced training for judges with administrative responsibilities. In addition, she worked in Kosovo, Romania and Haiti. Prior to working on contracts to USAID and the World Bank, Virginia worked 10 years for the Colorado Judicial Department where she was responsible for the training of judges, magistrates, court clerks and probation officers. Her educational background is in curriculum and instruction.

Summer Lopez serves as the **Deputy Regional Coordinator for the Middle East and Asia** and is temporarily in an acting role as Regional Coordinator for the Middle East on the **Global and Regional Policy Team**. She is also **Co-Chair of the DRG Gender Working Group**. Summer joined USAID as a Presidential Management Fellow and has done rotations at the State Department and at USAID/Nepal. She was closely involved in the development of the U.S. National Action Plan on Women, Peace, and Security, and acts as Activity Manager for the DRG Center's Global Women's Leadership Fund program. Before joining USAID, Summer was Vice President of Operations for The AjA Project, an international nonprofit based in California that works with refugee youth. She has previously worked with CARE International in India and in Ghana, where she evaluated a program on local governance and community-level capacity building. Summer has conducted field research on security sector reform and electoral processes in Liberia, Sierra Leone, and Sudan, and spent three years teaching at the American International School in Egypt. She holds a Bachelor of Arts in English from Harvard University and a Master of Public Affairs in International Development from the Woodrow Wilson School of Public and International Affairs at Princeton University.

Leah Maxson serves as a **Technical Advisor** for disability under the **Vulnerable Populations** portfolio within the **Human Rights Team**. In this role, she works to advance disability inclusion and further inclusive development programs and practices within the Agency and its missions. Leah also manages the DRG Disability funding. Her assistance to the field includes reviewing mission orders and strategies to promote disability inclusion; helping to design disability inclusive projects and activities; linking missions with disability experts in their countries or regions; and providing general resources for all things disability.

Tess McEnery is a **Democracy Specialist** in the **Elections and Political Transitions Team**. Tess serves as the EPT regional coordinator for Western and Central Africa. She also provides special coverage for the West Africa Regional Mission and all associated non-presence countries, such as Cote d'Ivoire. Tess is the AOR for the Consortium for Electoral and Political Processes Strengthening (**CEPPS III**) procurement mechanism. Tess has technical expertise in the field of electoral violence and conflict; she manages the Electoral Security initiative, which includes the USAID Electoral Security Framework and the Electoral Security Best Practices Guide. As the training coordinator for the EPT team, Tess delivers both general and specific training modules on the Electoral Security Framework. Prior to working on Africa, Tess focused on EPT issues in Eastern Europe, and she has worked in places as diverse as Kosovo and Sierra Leone. Tess previously worked as a North Atlantic Treaty Organization (NATO) Defense Policy Officer and Georgia Desk Officer at the State Department. Tess holds a M.P.A from the Maxwell School at Syracuse University, and she earned her BA in Political Science from Guilford College.

Kendra Miller is the **Travel Specialist** on the **Strategic Planning Team**. Prior to joining the DRG Center, Kendra worked in DCHA's Office of Civilian Military Cooperation (OCMC) as the Program Support Assistant. In this position, she managed senior staff calendars, facilitated personnel issues, managed and tracked OE, coordinated travel and daily events as well as acted as the lead on all administrative and logistical issues. Kendra has a Bachelor's degree in Sociology and Political Science from Claflin University, and she is currently pursuing a Master's degree in Human Resource Development from Bowie State University. Kendra has worked with USAID since August 2012.

Lisa McGregor-Mirghani is a **Democracy Officer** focused on Local Solutions and DRG Integration on the **Cross-Sectoral Program Team**. She is a Foreign Service Officer and previously served as the Local Capacity Team and Development Leadership Initiative Coordinator for USAID/East Africa. Prior to joining USAID, Ms. McGregor-Mirghani worked for 12 years as a private consultant to non-governmental organizations and local government in the areas of program design, project management, best practice research, evaluation, and fundraising. She also worked for 10 years in management and project implementation positions with CARE International, UNDP and the International Rescue Committee in Bangladesh, Thailand and the Sudan. Ms.

McGregor-Mirghani has a Master's in International Affairs and a Master's in Urban Planning from Columbia University.

Carrie Mitchell is currently serving as the **Latin America Regional Coordinator** on the **Strategic Planning and Research Team**. Carrie provides DRG support to the fifteen Missions in Latin America and the Caribbean, specifically backstopping Honduras, and represents the DRG office and USAID in strategy and budget discussions. Prior to joining DCHA/DRG, Carrie served in the Asia Bureau, providing support to the Central Asia Mission and the Bangladesh Mission. Carrie also served in USAID/Nicaragua in the Program Office and the Democracy Office, where she managed the elections program. Carrie holds a JD/MA from American University and a bachelor's degree in International Affairs and Russian from the George Washington University.

William Mishler is the **Senior Survey Research Specialist** with the DRG Learning Team. A Democracy Fellow, he is on leave from the University of Arizona where he is Professor of Government and Public Policy specializing in Democratization, Public Opinion, and Research Method /Statistics. Bill earned his PhD and learned his jump-shot at Duke University. He is the author of eight books and more than 60 articles on mass political behavior most recently focusing on the dynamics of popular support for both democratic and authoritarian regimes. Bill served on two occasions as Political Science Program Director at the National Science Foundation and worked briefly in the office of Congressman Claude Pepper (D, Fla.).

Jill Moss is **DRG's Digit Media, ICT and Internet Freedom Fellow**. In this role, she helps assess and design CSM programs, focusing specifically on the integration of information and communication technologies (ICT) in civil society and among independent media. While at USAID missions overseas, Jill also provides digital security and privacy support to indigenous journalists, activists and civil society groups. She is also a social media and social network analyst with the technical skills to leverage big data for visualization and evaluative work. Prior to becoming a Democracy Fellow, Jill was a member the Broadcasting Board of Governors' Internet Anti-Censorship Team -- a critical program for distributing US international broadcast elements (VOA, RFERL, RFA, MBN & OCB) into denied cyber environments. Jill is also a doctoral student studying strategic communication at George Mason University. Her research interests include ICT diffusion and adoption, business models for journalistic start-ups and mobile technology. In addition, she has taught journalism and radio news as an adjunct in the GMU Communication Department. Her pedagogical approach is based on 12 years reporting experience with the Voice of America. Jill started her career on Capitol Hill working as press secretary for her Nebraska Congressman. She's been involved in several political campaigns, and served as a United States Peace Corps volunteer from 1997 to 1999. She has a double-major B.A. in journalism and communication studies from the University of Iowa, and an M.A. in international education from GMU.

Laura Pavlovic is the **Team Leader** of the **Cross-Sectoral Programs team** in the DRG Center. She joined USAID in 2005. Prior to her arrival in Washington in September, Laura served as the director of the Office of Democracy and Governance at USAID's regional mission in Ukraine. In Ukraine, she was responsible for the implementation of Ukraine's $44.9 million MCC Threshold Program, and designed and managed programs in anti-corruption, legislative strengthening, rule of law, civil society and elections and political processes. Laura previously served as a Crisis, Stabilization and Governance Officer with USAID Washington, serving as acting Desk Officer for Ukraine, Moldova and Belarus, and also working on rule of law, counter-terrorism and legislative strengthening programming in Africa, Latin America and Eastern Europe. She also served as the USAID Burundi Program Manager based in Nairobi, Kenya, where she managed the development and implementation of USAID's post-conflict development program in Burundi. Prior to joining USAID, Laura worked as a program advisor for the Kenya Human Rights Commission, where she focused on housing rights and participatory budgeting processes, and as a corporate attorney in New York and Washington, where she also worked extensively on human rights and political asylum issues. Laura has also worked for the Office of the Prosecutor of the International Criminal

Tribunal for the former Yugoslavia. She has a J.D. from Harvard Law School and a B.A. in Slavic Languages and Literatures from the University of Pennsylvania.

Kristin Poore is a **Crisis, Stabilization and Governance Officer** focused on Vulnerable Populations programs on the **Human Rights Team**. Ms. Poore has a range of professional experience stretching across rule of law, human rights, civil society strengthening, conflict mitigation, humanitarian assistance and food security. Ms. Poore has worked in Jordan, Central Asia and the Democratic Republic of the Congo and holds a Master's in International Relations from Johns Hopkins University's School for Advanced International Studies (SAIS).

Heela Rasool is a **Crisis, Stabilization and Governance Officer** serving on the **Cross-Sectoral Programs Team**, focusing on health integration. She will be working to support missions and other USAID bureaus and operating units in the design, implementation and evaluation of programs to integrate DRG considerations and practices in the health sector. Ms. Rasool's professional experiences include: program design and management; local capacity development; conflict mitigation; anti-corruption; fraud investigations; social accountability assessments; humanitarian needs assessments; procurement transparency; corporate ethics and compliance. She has worked in Afghanistan, India, Bangladesh, Nepal and Ethiopia.

Corinne Rothblum serves on the **Cross-Sectoral Programs Team** as a **Democracy Specialist**. Her primary focus is to support missions and other USAID bureaus and operating units in the design, implementation and evaluation of programs to (1) strengthen partner country systems and (2) integrate DRG considerations and practices in USAID's other socio-economic sectors. Ms. Rothlum also has a range of professional experience conducting legislative and policy research and analysis, managing public-private partnerships, and evaluating land use planning issues from an economic development perspective, as well as experience designing and managing programs to improve the effectiveness, transparency and responsiveness of local governance. Ms. Rothblum has worked in Central/Eastern Europe; the Balkans; Asia; Africa; the Middle East; and the Caribbean.

Caroline Sahley Ph.D. joined USAID in 2002 and currently serves as a **Democracy Specialist** in the **Elections and Political Transitions Team**. Carol provides technical assistance to Missions in the design, implementation and evaluation of election and political party programs, with a particular focus on Africa. Carol's main areas of interest include parallel vote tabulations, election observation, electoral violence prevention and electronic voting systems. She previously served in the Civil Society Team, and has experience with civil society development and civic education. At that time, she led an initiative on cross-sectoral programming and designed a framework to assess and understand the links between governance and food security. Carol also served as the DRG Center's Co-chair of the Policy Task Team that developed the 2013 DRG Strategy.

Cathy Savino works with the Vulnerable Populations portfolio housed within the **Human Rights Team**. This primarily includes funds related to the Displaced Children and Orphans, the Leahy War Victims, Victims of Torture, wheelchairs and disability. Under the leadership of Rob Horvath, the Vulnerable Populations' team can provide information on fund guidelines, accessing technical assistance and pending competitive procurements.

Keith Schulz is **a Democracy Specialist** in the **Governance and Rule of Law Team,** where he focuses on legislative strengthening issues. He provides technical advice and assistance on governance programs in general and more specifically evaluates, assesses, monitors, designs, and trains on legislative strengthening programs and strategies. Keith has extensive experience working in the Middle East, Africa, Eastern Europe and Asia, and currently backstops Libya. Keith is also the DRG Office's liaison to the House Democracy Assistance Commission of the U.S. Congress. Prior to working for USAID, Keith spent three years as the senior technical advisor for a USAID-funded legislative strengthening program with the Palestinian Legislative Council in West Bank/Gaza and one year in Cambodia as a legal advisor to the Cambodia National Assembly's Center for Legal Research and

Documentation. Keith also worked for five years as a legislative counsel for the California State Legislature and, before that, as law clerk to United States District Court Judge Robert Broomfield in Phoenix, Arizona. He has a law degree from the University of San Diego, School of Law, where he was Lead Articles Editor of the San Diego Law Review, a B.A. from Tufts University, and a Master's Degree in International Policy and Practice from The George Washington University. Keith also attended McGill University in Montreal.

Lauren Seyfried is a **Program Analyst** with the **Strategic Planning Team**. Lauren supports the DRG Center on executive and program management and policy analysis. Lauren coordinates closely for the DRG Center with the DCHA Front Office as well as OTI and CMM. Lauren is a member of the DRG Center's Gender Working Group, and the DRG Strategy Implementation Working Group. Formerly a Presidential Management Fellow, Lauren served as a program officer in the Regional Development Mission for Asia in Bangkok, Thailand, a communications specialist in the Bureau for Management; and a program officer at USAID/Haiti. Lauren holds a Master's in Public Policy from Georgetown University and a Bachelor's degree in Political Science and Philosophy from Boston College.

Andrew Solomon is a **Democracy Fellow** on the **Human Rights Team** where he serves as a transitional justice advisor. A subject matter expert in justice and security sector assistance, Andrew has extensive experience directing technical assistance activities, performing assessments, and conducting field-work throughout Europe, Central and South Asia, Africa, and the Middle East. His work is currently focused on developing technical tools to prevent and respond to mass atrocities and human rights abuses. Previously, Andrew drafted rule of law program management doctrine at State/INL through BlueLaw International and led evaluations of criminal justice programs in Afghanistan and Kosovo. He was also a Fellow at the Brookings Institution, where he formally advised the United Nations Secretary General's Representative on Internal Displacement. At ABA/CEELI, Andrew directed research and oversaw assessments. Andrew also worked in the legal departments of the Office of the High Representative in Bosnia and the United Nations High Commissioner for Refugees. In addition, he has participated in more than fifteen election observation missions in Europe and Eurasia for the OSCE and IFES. Andrew holds a J.D. from Catholic University, an M.A. from American University, and a B.A. from Temple University.

Kevin Sturr is the **Human Rights Team leader**. Prior to joining the DRG Office, Kevin served as the Director of USAID/Bangladesh's Office of Democracy and Governance, and before that as Director of USAID Zimbabwe's Office of Democracy and Governance. In Zimbabwe, Kevin managed a legislative strengthening program, a civil society grants-making program, an agreement with a local organization for the provision of medical and psycho-social care and treatment for victims of organized violence and torture, and two other local agreements with a lawyers' human rights organization and with a local think tank. Before his DRG work, Kevin spent a tour in Senegal working in the West Africa Regional Food for Peace Office and managed grants in 4 Sahelian countries. Prior to joining USAID, Kevin worked for seven years in the Sahel including in Mauritania, Mali, Burkina Faso, Niger and Chad, as a Food Security analyst. Kevin was a Peace Corps Volunteer in Mali. He is fluent in French and also speaks 2 West African languages, Fulfuldé and Bambara. Kevin has a Bachelor's Degree in Political Science from Columbia University and a Masters from Tulane University. He also studied public interest law at City University of New York.

Sarah Swift serves at **Project Development Officer** within the **Cross-Sectoral Programs Team**. Prior to joining the DRG Center, she served within the Africa Bureau, working first as a Desk Officer for Liberia and Sierra Leone, and then within the Bureau's program office. Within the program office, she supported both CDCS development, and engaged substantially on regional programs, including as the backstop of the Agency's nascent African Union program. Prior to Africa bureau, she worked on Donor Coordination within the former bureau for Policy and Program Coordination. Sarah received an MPA in International Relations from the Woodrow Wilson

School at Princeton University, and a Bachelor's Degree in Political Science and Peace Studies from Haverford College.

Joe Taggart serves as the **Team leader** for the **Strategic Planning Team**, coordinating the Center's strategic planning and budgeting processes. Joe formerly served as the Senior Democracy and Governance Advisor for USAID/Caucasus/Mission where he contributed to the development of DRG programs in Georgia including the period of Georgia's "Rose Revolution"; as the Officer-in-Charge for USAID's programs in Montenegro which included Montenegro's successful referendum for independence from Serbia; and as the Chief of the Democracy and Governance Office for USAID/Azerbaijan. Prior to joining USAID in 2001 Joe worked with a USAID DRG implementing partner in the Caucasus, served as a presidential political appointee in the Department of Agriculture as a senior liaison from Secretary Dan Glickman's office with state and local elected officials and as a Senior District Aide for Rep. Glickman (D-KS).

Jeffrey Vanness serves as **Democracy and Governance Field Advisor** on the **Elections and Political Transitions Team**. Jeff engages USAID field missions, other USG entities, and the broader democracy and governance community on issues related to elections, political competition, governance, and consensus building. Prior to joining USAID in 2011 as Senior Governance Advisor for USAID/Bangladesh, he worked for the International Republican Institute (IRI) in Morocco, Bangladesh, and Timor Leste; for the Center for International Private Enterprise (CIPE); and for the Organization for Security and Cooperation in Europe (OSCE). He began his career as a legislative aide to two members of the U.S. Congress and later worked on political campaigns in his native Tennessee. Jeff studied international affairs at George Washington University and earned a master's degree from the Massachusetts Institute of Technology.

Julie Werbel is a **Senior Security Sector Reform (SSR) Advisor** on the **Governance and Rule of Law Team.** She provides technical assistance and advice on security sector governance, rule of law, policing, defense, and civil-military relations to foreign governments, USAID Missions, and the US interagency. She served as an advisor to the US Security Coordinator for Middle East Peace in Jerusalem and has conducted SSR, fragile state, and governance assessments in Africa, Asia and Latin America. She speaks French. Previously, Julie was a Principal at DFI Government Services, a Washington, DC-based defense consulting firm. At DFI, she conducted analyses for the Office of the Secretary of Defense (OSD) relating to political-military strategy, peacetime military engagement, civil-military relations, NATO enlargement, and stability operations. Julie also served as the Program Manager and Director of Participant Affairs for the Africa Center for Strategic Studies (ACSS), a DoD regional center that she designed and helped to establish. Her career includes service with the Peace Corps and U.S. Department of State and business research for the New York-based Conference Board. Julie has worked in more than two dozen countries on four continents. She earned an M.A. in Law and Diplomacy from the Fletcher School of Law and Diplomacy and a Bachelor's degree from Cornell University.

Sara Werth is the **Team Leader** for **Governance and Rule of Law** in the Center of Excellence on Democracy, Human Rights and Governance. Ms. Werth joined USAID in 2006 as the Senior Governance and Elections Advisor at the Mission in Bangladesh where she managed political party strengthening, elections and anti-corruption projects. She joined USAID as a career Foreign Service Officer in 2008 and was assigned to the Office of Vulnerable Populations in Colombia. She supported the demobilization and reintegration of ex-combatants as well as the design of Colombia's first Afro-Colombian and Indigenous program. In September 2010, she became the Deputy Director of the Democracy and Governance Office in Guatemala and designed and managed violence prevention and security and justice sector reform projects. Prior to joining USAID, Ms. Werth worked for the International Republican Institute and the Civic Education Project, a Soros-funded organization. She has a Master's degree in international relations from the School of Advanced International Studies at Johns Hopkins University and served as a Peace Corps Volunteer in Lithuania from 1997-1999.

Chris White is a **Program Officer** on the Center's **Strategic Planning Team**, responsible for the Center's budget and financial management as well as strategic communications on budget-related activities. He also serves as the Center's country backstop on South Sudan. Chris is a former Presidential Management Fellow and enlisted Marine with policy experience in the Department of Homeland Security and the Office of the Under Secretary of Defense for Policy (Pakistan Desk).

Nicole Widdersheim joined the **Human Rights Team** as a **Human Rights Advisor** in January 2014 and is the **Fund Manager for the Human Rights Grants Program**. She also backstops work on Atrocity Prevention. Recently, Nicole has served as the USAID Office of Transition Initiative (OTI) Country Representative in Cote d'Ivoire, Mali and Haiti and as USAID Protection Officer in Darfur, Sudan. She can support missions in working with local partners and organizations. She can support designing small grant components within larger programs, and designing human rights, humanitarian and community stability programming. She has conducted PPRs and other assessments of USAID and partner programming. She has experience managing large contractors and working with wide variety of sub-contractors and government partners. Being field-based for the bulk of her career, she is adept at working in insecure and fast-paced environments with many stakeholders with which to coordinate and many security protocols to follow. She has represented OTI in the agency working groups on operating in Non-Permissive Environments and Preventing Atrocities. She also has experience in managing and implementing emergency reconstruction, media programming, workforce development, elections and transitional justice programs. Short assignments have included work in Ethiopia, Rwanda, Bosnia and Afghanistan. She has a MA in Human Rights and Political Theory from University of Essex, UK and is conversational in French and familiar with Arabic.

John Williamson is **Senior Technical Advisor** for the **Displaced Children and Orphans Fund (DCOF)**. DCOF supports programs for especially vulnerable children, especially those who are outside of family care or at high risk of losing family care. This includes children in residential care, on the street, separated by armed conflict or disaster, former child soldiers, or otherwise without adequate family care. For DCOF, he assesses situations involving such children, identifies relevant interventions, and assesses projects. He is one of the organizers of the Better Care Network and the Washington Network for Children and Armed Conflict. He has written or collaborated in writing publications on alternative care, child soldiers, children affected by HIV/AIDS, and psychosocial issues among conflict-affected populations. He has a master's degree in social work.

Lawrence Woocher is **Senior Atrocity Prevention Fellow** working with the **Human Rights Team**. He is contributing to USAID's work on the comprehensive U.S. government strategy to prevent and respond to mass atrocities, which President Obama announced in April 2012. Lawrence has been working on early warning, conflict prevention, and the prevention of genocide and mass atrocities for more than a decade. Prior to his USAID fellowship, he was research director of the Political Instability Task Force at Science Applications International Corporation (SAIC). From 2006-2011, he was a senior program officer at the United States Institute of Peace (USIP). While at USIP, he was a member of the executive committee and lead expert on early warning for the Genocide Prevention Task Force, co-chaired by former Secretary of State Madeleine Albright and former Secretary of Defense William Cohen. Before joining USIP, Woocher was a research fellow at Columbia University's Center for International Conflict Resolution and, concurrently, a consultant on early warning to the Office of the Special Adviser to the UN Secretary-General on the Prevention of Genocide. Lawrence is also a lecturer at the Elliott School of International Affairs at George Washington University. He received a Master's in Public Policy from Harvard's Kennedy School and a Bachelor's in Neuroscience from Brown University.

Maryanne Yerkes currently serves as a **Democracy Specialist** with the **Civil Society and Media Team**. Her areas of expertise include civil society and post-conflict reconstruction, youth and conflict, and civic education.

The countries she backstops are Nigeria and Guinea. In addition to her regular work, which includes providing technical leadership on civil society issues, assisting Missions in designs, assessments, and evaluations of civil society programs, Maryanne also engages in interagency working groups on issues such as reconstruction and stabilization. Prior to joining USAID, Maryanne worked with and consulted for various non-governmental organizations and research institutes focused on peace building and development, including the United States Institute of Peace, Pax Christi International, and Oxfam America. She also completed a fellowship in the Balkans focused on transitional justice. Maryanne holds an M.A in International Peace and Conflict Resolution from American University and a B.A. in International Studies and French from the University of North Carolina at Chapel Hill. She speaks French fluently and has some competency in Spanish and Bosnian/Serbian/Croatian.

Veronica Zeitlin works on **Counter-Trafficking In Persons** on the **Human Rights Team** in the DRG Center. She coordinates DCHA's anti-trafficking activities and is **co-chair** of the interagency anti-trafficking Grant Making Committee. Before transitioning to DRG, she managed trafficking and gender programs in the Agency's Office of Women in Development. Prior to USAID, she covered Africa at the State Department's Office to Monitor and Combat Trafficking in Persons, where she monitored trafficking in 25 countries though frequent in-country assessments and worked with foreign government officials and NGOs to combat it. Before the State Department, Ms. Zeitlin managed women's political participation projects in West Africa at the National Democratic Institute and, while based in Dakar, Senegal, consulted for USAID, UNICEF, and Refugees International on human rights issues. Prior to transitioning to the public sector, she practiced law at Hughes Hubbard & Reed. She holds a B.A. in Anthropology from Columbia University and a J.D. from the University of Virginia.

BIOGRAPHIES—REGIONAL DRG TECHNICAL EXPERTS

Africa

Kellie Burk works for the **U.S. Agency for International Development (USAID) Bureau for Africa as a Democracy and Governance Specialist**. As a democracy and conflict research analyst she supports the team in developing products and presentations. Prior to arriving at USAID in 2009, Ms. Burk worked at the Academy for Educational Development (AED), where she served for several years as a researcher for the now defunct USAID Africa Bureau Information Center (ABIC), as well as a manager for various civil society capacity building projects. She earned her MA in African Studies from Johns Hopkins University-SAIS, consulted at the World Bank and IFES, and previously worked and lived in East Africa as a trade finance specialist. Kellie can be reached at kburk@usaid.gov.

Ryan McCannell works for the **U.S. Agency for International Development (USAID) Bureau for Africa as a Democracy and Governance Specialist**. Before joining USAID in 2004, Mr. McCannell spent eight years at the National Democratic Institute for International Affairs (NDI), where he was responsible for designing and managing democracy support programs in Nigeria, Côte d'Ivoire, Burkina Faso, Sierra Leone, Malawi, South Africa, and the Central African Republic. In 2002-03, he served as NDI's chief of party in Benin and Togo, where he organized training for political parties prior to elections in those two countries. Before NDI, he worked for the Academy for Educational Development (AED) as a democracy researcher for USAID. His education includes a bachelor's degree at Georgetown's School of Foreign Service, a year abroad at the Université du Bénin in Lomé, Togo, and a master's in Geographic and Cartographic Sciences at George Mason University. Ryan can be reached at rmccannell@usaid.gov.

Jeremy Meadows is a **Democracy Specialist in the USAID Bureau for Africa**. He provides advice and support to USAID Missions in Africa on the range of democracy and governance subsectors, with a particular emphasis on parliamentary strengthening, governance, and civil society issues. Before joining USAID in December 2008, Mr. Meadows spent thirteen and a half years at the National Conference of State Legislatures (NCSL). In addition to developing and managing NCSL's State- and USAID-funded exchange and technical assistance programs with legislative bodies in Africa and the Middle East, he also worked on a variety of state-federal policy issues, ranging from immigration, immigrants, and refugees to agriculture, housing, and economic development. He concluded his tenure at NCSL as the organization's lobbyist for international trade and transportation issues. Jeremy worked closely and regularly with state legislators, legislative staff, congressional staff, foreign parliamentarians and parliamentary staff, as well as a range federal officials. His Bachelor's in Politics & French is from Washington & Lee University and his Master's in International Political Economy is from the University of Kentucky's Patterson School. Jeremy can be reached at jmeadows@usaid.gov.

Asia/Middle East

April Hahn works in the **Asia/Middle East Bureau** as the **Chief of the Democracy, Governance, and Conflict Team**. Previously, she was the Regional Coordinator for Latin America and the Caribbean on the Strategic Planning and Research Division in the DRG Office. Her geographical experience includes Latin America, Asia and Middle East. Her country backstops in the DRG Office are Cuba and Ecuador. She has working knowledge of Spanish. April also served as the Asia and Near East Coordinator on the Election and Political Process Division and as backstop for Afghanistan and Pakistan. April holds a Ph.D. from the University of Virginia in International Relations. April can be reached at ahahn@usaid.gov .

Dr. Gavin Helf is currently a **Senior Democracy and Governance Advisor** in the **Asia/ Middle East** bureaus covering Central and South Asia. He has been closely involved in the USAID response to the 2010 Revolution in Kyrgyzstan. Gavin worked at USAID/Iraq, managing and helping design and procure much of the COIN and democracy and governance portfolio there. He studied, lived and worked in the USSR and its successor states, and was a democracy and governance advisor at USAID/Armenia. Prior, Gavin was Director of Grant Programs for the Eurasia Foundation and was the Central Asia Regional Director for the International Research & Exchanges Board based in Almaty. Gavin has taught Russian and Soviet foreign policy and comparative politics at Notre Dame, Cornell and Moscow's International University and worked for Radio Liberty as a Soviet area research specialist in the late 1980s. He received in Ph.D. in political science from UC Berkeley in 1994. Gavin can be reached at ghelf@usaid.gov .

Dara Katz is currently a **Democracy Specialist**, serving as a senior advisor on democracy, governance, peace and security issues in the **Middle East**. Before joining the Middle East Bureau, Dara was a Civilian Response Corps member, working with the Rule of Law team and in an inter-agency engagement in Southern Sudan. She has spent more than a decade in conflict and post-conflict zones (Afghanistan, Pakistan, Kosovo, Bosnia) working on a broad range of DRG issues. Prior to her field work, she co-founded and managed an NGO working on US policy towards the Balkans, Network Bosnia. She also has worked with International Rescue Committee in Pakistan and supported US Army trainings related to Afghanistan. Dara is the author of the two-volume UNAMA-OHCHR report, *Arbitrary Detention in Afghanistan: A Call to Action,* co-author of "Returning to Basics: Property Rights in South-East Europe" in Hernando de Soto and Francis Cheneval (eds), Realizing Property Rights and of OMiK, *Property Rights in Kosovo 2002-2003* as well as other public reports. She holds a BA with Honors from Wesleyan University and an LLM with Distinction in International Human Rights Law from the University of Essex. Dara can be reached at dkatz@usaid.gov .

Oliver Wilcox is **Senior Democracy, Governance and Conflict Advisor** in the **Middle East Bureau**, where he develops strategies and programming and shapes interagency planning and coordination for the region on democracy/governance, youth, Muslim engagement, counter-extremism and stabilization. Previously, Oliver was an Adjunct Instructor at the University of Virginia and Trinity College in Washington, DC. He was also a Senior Editor for the *Arab Studies Journal*; an American Center for Oriental Research Fellow in Jordan, where he researched political liberalization; and a Fulbright Scholar in Spain, where he studied European Maghreb policies. Oliver completed Ph.D. studies and earned an M.A. in Political Science from the University of Virginia, as well as an M.A. with a distinction in Arab Studies from Georgetown University. He graduated with honors and special honors in Political Science and Spanish from Tufts University. Oliver can be reached at owilcox@usaid.gov.

Europe and Eurasia
Suren Avanesyan is the **Senior Rule of Law Advisor** in the **Europe and Eurasia Bureau.** In this role, Suren provides technical guidance and policy advice to the Bureau, the field missions and the US Government on issues relating to the justice sector reform efforts in the former Soviet Union and the countries of Eastern and Central Europe. Prior to joining USAID, he worked in several for-profit and not-for-profit international development organizations in Washington, DC, where he designed, implemented, assessed and evaluated rule of law programs in Eastern Europe, Africa and Asia. Suren was a home office director of the USAID Justice Sector Reform Activity—a project that saw the transition of Kosovo from an international protectorate to an independent country resulting in creation of the brand new Ministry of Justice and Judicial Council. He also managed projects in Serbia, Azerbaijan, Mongolia and Egypt and worked on ROL assessments and evaluations in, *inter alia*, Russia, Bosnia and Herzegovina, Montenegro, Albania, Ukraine, Georgia, Serbia and Sub-Saharan Africa. A native of Russia, Suren practiced law in Russia as a member of the Union of Advokats of Russia, and is fluent in Russian. Suren completed his MA (1998) and JD (1999) at the University of Wisconsin-Madison and LL.M. in International Legal Studies (2001) at New York University School of Law. He has published articles on international human and constitutional rights, child trafficking, and issues of civil liability in international law. Suren can be reached at savanesyan@usaid.gov.

Meg Gaydosik is the **Senior Media Development/Rights and Tolerance Advisor** in the **Europe and Eurasia Bureau** at USAID/Washington. In this capacity, Meg provides advice and assistance to USAID Missions on indigenous media development programming and freedom of expression/access to information issues. Prior to joining USAID in 2006, She worked for 11 years as an on-site media development consultant and/or project manager in nearly all of the Balkan and former Soviet Union countries. Meg was awarded a Knight International Press Fellowship (2003-2004), serving in Hungary, Romania and Slovakia. She is a former commercial television station manager from Fairbanks, Alaska. Meg has a B.S. in Art Education from Edinboro State University and can be reached at mgaydosik@usaid.gov.

Erin McCarthy is a **Democracy Specialist** for the **Democracy and Governance Team** in the **Bureau for Europe and Eurasia.** In this capacity, she serves as the primary backstop for the sector Advisors and assists in the management of several regional programs. Prior to joining USAID in February of 2009, Erin earned her M.A. in International Commerce and Policy from George Mason University and her B.A. in International Relations and French from James Madison University. She also holds a professional certification in Conflict Reconstruction, Stabilization, and Prevention at George Mason's Institute for Conflict Analysis and Resolution. Erin can be reached at emccarthy@usaid.gov .

Alexander Sokolowski serves as the **Democracy and Governance Team Leader** of the **Bureau for Europe and Eurasia** at USAID/Washington. In this capacity, he provides advice and technical assistance on elections assistance and political party development. Prior to joining USAID in June 2003, Alex taught Comparative Politics at George Washington University as an adjunct professor. He received his Ph.D. in Politics from Princeton University in November 2002, writing his dissertation on the structural and political determinants of fiscal and social policy failure in Yeltsin's Russia. Alex has served as a Foreign Policy Research Fellow at the Brookings Institution (2000-2001). He also holds master's degrees from Princeton (2000) and the Fletcher School of Law and Diplomacy (1994). Alex previously worked for the National Democratic Institute's Moscow office as a Political Party Program Officer and Political Analyst. Fluent in Russian, he has published articles on Russian politics in academic journals (*Europe-Asia Studies, Demokratizatsiya*) and opinion pieces (*The Moscow Times*). Alex can be reached at asokolowski@usaid.gov.

Latin America and the Caribbean

Eric Kite is USAID's **Democracy Team Leader** for **Latin America and the Caribbean (LAC).** He has also served as an anti-corruption advisor, then LAC strategies coordinator in the Democracy & Governance Office. Eric also previously led USAID's Democracy Office in Afghanistan. He has degrees in political science and German from the University of Missouri, a Fulbright from Bonn University, and an M.A. with emphasis in democratic transitions from Georgetown University. Eric can be reached at ekite@usaid.gov .

E. Brennan Dorn works on the **Democracy and Human Rights Team** of the **Bureau for Latin America and the Caribbean**. Her graduate studies at the Gerald R. Ford School of Public Policy of the University of Michigan focused on international security and the developing world. During graduate school, Brennan interned in the Department of Human and Trade Union Rights at Education International, the global trade union federation for educators. Prior to earning her master's degree and subsequently joining USAID, she was a field organizer for the United Faculty of Florida, a higher education professionals' union. During her undergraduate studies in Sociology at Georgetown University, she spent a year studying in Brazil, where she worked on issues of social education for underprivileged children. Brennan can be reached at ebdorn@usaid.gov.

Danielle Reiff is a **Foreign Service Officer**, who has served as a Program Officer and a Democracy and Governance Officer with USAID. Danielle currently works on the USAID program, based in Washington D.C., to strengthen civic participation in Cuba. Prior, she managed USAID support to the Juba peace process and post-conflict transition in northern Uganda. She also managed USAID support to Uganda's transition to multiparty politics, including observation of the historic multiparty elections of 2006, Parliamentary strengthening, local government capacity building and increasing civic participation in elected governance institutions. Prior to joining USAID, Danille worked for the UN Department of Peacekeeping Operations and the World Bank's Conflict Prevention and Reconstruction Unit. She was a U.S. Peace Corps volunteer in Burkina Faso. Danielle was a member of the first ever class of Rotary World Peace Fellows and earned a Master's degree in Peace Studies and Development at the Institute of Political Studies (Sciences Po) in Paris, France. Danielle can be reached at dreiff@usaid.gov.

Vanessa Reilly is **a Democracy Specialist** in the **Bureau for Latin America and the Caribbean**, where she focuses on elections, civil society and governance. She manages agreements to support election commissions and electoral observation and to conduct the "Americas Barometer" surveys of democratic attitudes and behaviors in the region. Vanessa worked in the DG office of USAID/Kenya and began her government service as a Presidential Management Fellow at the Department of State. She has worked with NGOs in Mexico, Honduras, Puerto Rico and Washington, DC. Vanessa speaks Spanish fluently and has an M.A. in International Development and International Economics from Johns Hopkins SAIS, a Master of Public Administration from Syracuse University's Maxwell School, and a B.A. in Political Science and Spanish from Ohio State University. Vanessa can be reached at vreilly@usaid.gov.

HOW TO ACCESS A DRG IMPLEMENTING MECHANISM

Sample statements of work are available from DRG staff. Please contact Valerie Hovetter at vhovetter@usaid.gov for more information.

Accessing an Indefinite Quantity Contract (IQC):

NOTE: There is no dollar value or time limit on delivery orders other than the IQC ceiling/period of performance.

1. To access an IQC, Missions prepare a statement of work (SOW) for a task order that briefly describes the purpose, background, objectives, desired tasks or activities, deliverables, evaluation or performance measures as appropriate, as well as a notional budget, time frame, and evaluation/selection criteria including weighting of each criteria. Missions should consider providing advance notice to IQC holders of their intention to request proposals.
2. The SOW must be shared with the DRG Contracting Officer's Representative (COR). The COR must review the prospective task order requirements or statement of work and agree that it complies with the SOW for the basic contract before the task order Contracting Officer (CO) may begin the fair opportunity process.
3. For IQCs, thresholds of task order ceilings determine the process of fair opportunity to be followed. Missions should specify which threshold is being used in the Request for Task Order Proposal (RFTOP), and thus what page limits apply.
   a. Task Orders (TO) up to $100,000: All holders will be asked for proposals not to exceed a 2-page cost proposal and a 3-page technical proposal.
   b. Task Orders between $100,000 and $2M: All holders will be asked for proposals not to exceed 2-page cost proposal and 10-page technical proposal. Past performance information may also be required but this is not part of the 10-page technical proposal limit.
   c. Task Orders for more than $2M: Two-page cost proposal and 10-page technical proposal may be used, but the CO may request whatever level of information s/he deems appropriate.
4. All IQC holders must be given a fair opportunity to be considered for task orders over $2,500, unless the CO determines that one of the following exceptions to the fair opportunity requirements applies:
   a. An urgent need exists, and seeking competition would result in unacceptable delays;
   b. Only one contractor is capable at the level of quality required because the requirement is unique or highly specialized;
   c. The task order must be issued on a sole source basis in the interest of economy and efficiency because it is a logical follow-on to an order already issued under the contract, provided that all awardees were given a fair opportunity to be considered for the original order;
   d. To satisfy contract minimum award obligations; or
   e. Small business set aside.
5. After review of the SOW by the DRG COR, the Mission sends a formal request to its COR to negotiate a task order under an IQC.

Accessing an Associate Award under a Leader With Associates (LWA) Grant or Cooperative Agreement:

The "Associate" award is a separate cooperative agreement negotiated, funded and managed by the field mission. Proposed programs must fit within the scope of the activities under the central "Leader" award. The Mission sends a draft program description to the DRG program contact who serves as the Agreement Officer's Representative (AOR) of the leader award. If the existing grant or cooperative agreement program scope accommodates the proposed activity, the AOR reviews the Mission program description, provides any comments or feedback and signs off on the award. The Mission then conducts the procurement action for the award.

Accessing a Grant or a Cooperative Agreement (CA):

NOTE: Proposed programs must fit within the scope of the activities funded by the central award. However, grantees and CAs may agree to extend their program in a given country or to initiate a program in a new country. Because grants and CAs are assistance instruments, USAID may not impose a particular activity, nor may it dictate which member of the CA shall implement a given program. Preferences, however, should be stated and will be forwarded to the CA by the AOR along with the draft program description.

1. The Mission sends a draft program description to the DRG program contact who serves as the AOR. A notional budget should be attached.
2. If the existing grant or cooperative agreement program scope accommodates the proposed activity, the AOR reviews the Mission program description with the grantee. With grantee agreement the AOR responds to the Mission, a funds transfer is arranged, and an incremental funding action is scheduled. If the Mission program description cannot be accommodated in the program description of the existing grant or cooperative agreement, the AOR assesses partner organization interest in the Mission program description and then, as necessary, requests negotiation of modification of the grant/cooperative agreement by the grants officer. This requires significantly more time.

CROSS-CUTTING SERVICES
(Program Areas 2.1-2.4)

DRG Analytical Services
Democracy Grants & Fellowship Program
DRG Learning, Evaluation and Research

IQCS FOR DEMOCRACY AND GOVERNANCE ANALYTICAL SERVICES

DRG Contact: Brian Hanley (COR, GRP) & Stephanie Molina (Alternate, GRP)

IQCs	Award Number	Expiration	Performance Period
ARD, Inc.	AID-OAA-I-10-00001	8/1/2015	8/1/2016
Management Systems International	AID-OAA-I-10-00002	8/1/2015	8/1/2016
Social Impact*	AID-OAA-I-10-00003	8/1/2015	8/1/2016
Democracy International*	AID-OAA-I-10-00004	8/1/2015	8/1/2016
International Resources Group	AID-OAA-I-10-00005	8/1/2015	8/1/2016

PURPOSE:

The purpose of this contract is to provide missions and USAID/Washington operating units with analytical services and support to inform the design, evaluation, and implementation of USAID-funded democracy and governance strategies and programs. Such services will ensure that DRG strategies, programs and activities, and monitoring and evaluation plans are based on in-depth, well-informed analysis; cutting-edge research; valid data; and best practices in the field of democracy and governance.

POSSIBLE WORK AREAS:

The contractor may be called upon by DCHA/DRG, missions, regional bureaus, and other central bureaus to provide the following analytical services.

(a) General and Sectoral DRG Assessments

General and sectoral DRG assessments could include, but are not limited to, the following:

- Conducting full-scale, multi-person, "general DRG assessments" that include the examination of all major functional DRG components and areas of USAID interest;
- Conducting single component or "sectoral DRG assessments" (e.g., rule of law, decentralization, elections, civil/military relations);
- Executing regional or multi-country DRG assessments, both general and sectoral; and,
- Creating a common analytical framework and methodology for the conduct of DRG assessments, both general and sectoral.

(b) DRG Strategy Development

Support for DRG strategy development could include, but is not limited to, the following:

- Developing long-term strategic plans, including DRG assistance objectives and targets of opportunity, or incorporating DRG strategies, principles, and approaches into an overall program portfolio;
- Formulating regional-level DRG strategies, programs, and action plans; and,
- Conceptualizing Agency-wide DRG strategies, programs, and action plans.

(c) Managing for DRG Results

Support for monitoring and evaluation of DRG efforts could include, but is not limited to, the following:

- Creating DRG indicators at the strategic (objective), sectoral (technical), and activity (implementation) levels;
- Designing data collection and analysis plans and methodologies to track achievement toward stated objectives;
- Refining DRG indicators to monitor progress and measure impact of DRG programs; and,
- Developing or revising performance management plans, results frameworks, and/or annual performance reports (or their functional equivalents), including objectives and indicators.

(d) DRG Program and Activity Design

Support for the development of DRG programs and/or activities could include, but is not limited to, the following:

- Designing or redesigning stand-alone, multi-component, or single component DRG programs or activities;
- Designing or redesigning programs or activities in other development sectors which have either a DRG component or in which DRG principles and strategies are to be incorporated;
- Providing specific information, such as best practices or data, to help with the design or redesign of DRG programs or activities; and,
- Preparing various design documents and requirements (e.g., concept papers, Scopes of Work, New Activity Designs, Activity Proposals, technical analyses, and activity protocols or authorizing documents), per the legal and policy considerations cited above.

(e) DRG Evaluation

DRG evaluations could include, but are not limited to, the following:

- Conducting evaluations of programs and activities at various points of design and implementation including initial, mid-term, and final evaluations;
- Designing and conducting impact evaluations of DRG programs and activities in a given country or sub-region; and,
- Analyzing data from cross-national impact evaluations within a specific sub-sector to draw conclusions about the impact of DRG programs and make recommendations for best practices within that sub-sector.

(f) Research and Special Studies

Support for research could include, but is not limited to, the following:

- Collecting new data and/or adapting existing data on USAID activities: inputs, outputs, outcomes, and impacts;
- Collecting and/or adapting data on political, economic, social, and other phenomena in USAID recipient and non-recipient countries;
- Developing indices to monitor DRG programming;
- Reviewing secondary source research, including desk studies, evaluations, analyses of best practices, and syntheses of other sources of relevant materials;
- Conducting primary source research, for example via case studies or general sectoral evaluations, in such areas as backsliding, patronage, corruption, or Islam and Democracy;
- Conducting studies pertaining to policy constraints, theoretical limitations, and systemic or sectoral problems;
- Translating research findings from above analyses into periodic reports that are intelligible to a policy audience, and that spell out practical, programmatic implications of the research for democracy assistance practitioners; and,
- Writing handbooks, manuals, and reference materials needed for program development, implementation, and monitoring and evaluation.

(g) Survey Research and New Methodologies

Support for survey research and other methodological approaches could include, but is not limited to, the following:

- Undertaking surveys;
- Assessing the feasibility of survey research in a given context and providing general assistance to missions interested in using survey data or undertaking surveys;
- Providing guidance on ensuring high quality and relevant research designs and findings;
- Analyzing survey data, and analyzing the validity of other methodological approaches in a particular context;
- Developing training materials, workshops, and other pedagogical/information dissemination products in the field of survey research and methodology; and,

- Developing and/or expanding online and Web-related capabilities in USAID to provide survey findings and data for further use by missions and other operating units.

(h) USAID Training and DCHA/DRG Networking

Support for DRG training, networking, and outreach could include, but is not limited to, the following:

- Developing and implementing a training program to increase the knowledge and skills of USAID personnel or that of cooperating partners or other donors;
- Providing fora for mission and bureau staff to exchange experiences and lessons learned. The fora could take a variety of forms, such as conferences, workshops, electronic distributions and video-conferencing, and could include partners, academics, sectoral specialists, and other donors;
- Facilitating or conducting workshops that bring together USAID staff with cooperating agencies including PVOs, NGOs, universities, consulting firms, etc., to discuss the Agency's DRG programs and the potential role of these partners in program and strategy implementation; and,
- Facilitating or conducting workshops and conferences to discuss issues and problems of common interest to USAID, its partners, other donors, and others concerned about DRG issues.

(g) Grant Management

Funds may be made available on a grant basis for institutional capacity building in the analytical areas listed above. In such cases, the contractor may be required to execute and/or administer grants under awarded task orders.

USAID POCs:

Brian Hanley, Tel. 202-712-1806, bhanley@usaid.gov ; Stephanie Molina, Tel. 202-712-5346, smolina@usaid.gov

CONTRACTORS

ARD, Inc.	Management Systems International	Social Impact*
Kathy Stermer	Stacy Stacks	Douglas Kerr
159 Bank St., Suite 300	600 Water Street, S.W.	2300 Clarendon Blvd, Suite 300
Burlington, VT 05401-1397	Washington, D.C. 20024	Arlington, VA 22201
Tel: (802) 658-3890	Tel: (202) 484-7170	Tel: (703) 465-1884
Fax: (802) 658-4247	Fax: (202) 488-0754	Fax:
Email: dgreen@ardinc.com	Email: sstacks@msi-inc.com	Email: dkerr@socialimpact.com
Web: www.ardinc.com	Web: www.msiworldwide.com	Web: www.socialimpact.com
Democracy International*	International Resources Group	
Glenn Cowan	Sandra Shuster	
4802 Montgomery Lane	1211 Connecticut Avenue, NW,	
Bethesda, MD 20814	Suite 700	
Tel: (301) 961-1660	Washington, DC 20036	
Fax: (301) 961-6605	Tel: (202) 289-0100	
Email:	Fax: (202) 289-7601	
gcowan@democracyinternational.com	Email: sshuster@irgltd.com	
Web:	Web: http://www.irgltd.com	
www.democracyinternational.com		

*This is a small business.

DEMOCRACY FELLOWSHIPS AND GRANTS PROGRAM

DRG Contact: Joseph Taggart (COR, SP)

Cooperative Agreement	Award Number	Expiration	Performance Period
Institute of International Education (IIE)	AID-OAA-A-12-00039	9/04/2017	N/A

PURPOSE:

The Democracy Fellowships and Grants Program (DFG) is intended to help develop a pool of committed democracy, conflict and humanitarian assistance professionals at the junior, mid- and senior-levels; to strengthen relations between USAID and academic, think-tank and research organizations; and to promote research and innovative solutions to democracy, human rights and governance programs.

POSSIBLE WORK AREAS:

DFG represents a continuation of Democracy Fellowship programs that have been implemented by the DRG Center and its predecessors for about 17 years. The expanded DFG program contains three primary components: fellowships; DRG learning and exchanges; and innovation and research grants.

Fellowships:

Fellows will be hired into the program as full-time, part-time, or for short-term appointments. Full-time fellows will be exceptional, highly motivated junior to senior –level professionals to be placed at USAID offices or Missions. The duration of regular full-time fellowships is two years with an option to extend annually for an additional two years after the first two year assignment. Part-time fellows can be hired for the same duration as regular full-time fellows but can work for USAID on a part-time basis while maintaining their existing positions at their home institution. Short-term fellows can be junior to senior level and may be recruited to work on specific research projects or policy papers. Duration of short-term fellowships can be six months to one year. Part-time and short-term fellowships are intended to offer USAID more flexibility when collaborating with academic and think-tank organizations as well as make it possible for talented and exceptional professionals who otherwise may not be able to become full-time fellows to gain experience with international development programs and contribute to advancing USAID goals. Fellowships will respond to a range of technical assistance needs and will assist USAID in global leadership efforts, research, and knowledge management. USAID Missions and Offices interested in sponsoring a Fellow should contact the COR for a detailed description of the cost structure.

Learning Exchanges

Learning exchanges consist of internships and a series of speakers and workshops. The prospective internship program is expected to help interns gain critical experience in the DRG sector. The DRG speaker series and workshop component will bring outside speakers to present at USAID supported events or organize workshops.

Innovation and Research Grants

DCHA/DRG will announce priority research areas through annual updates of its Innovations and Research APS. The APS portfolio will foster and nurture ideas and projects that have the potential to lead to innovative solutions that may lead to significant advances in democracy, human rights and governance foreign assistance programs. Innovation and Research Grants will support projects in all sub-sectors of democracy, human rights and governance. Missions and Offices may also partner with the DRG Center to fund research and innovation grants either by funding existing broad calls for proposals or proposing their own topics for consideration for future grant solicitations.

USAID POC:

Joe Taggart, Tel. 202-712-0172, jtaggart@usaid.gov

GRANTEE:

Institute of International Education (IIE)

Lisa Peterson, Director, Democracy Fellows Program
1400 K Street NW, Washington, DC, 20005
E-mail: dem.fellows@iie.org Web: http://www.iie.org/Programs/USAID-Democracy-Fellows-and-Grants-Program
Telephone: +1 202.326.7759 Fax: +1 202.326.7754

DRG LEARNING, EVALUATION AND RESEARCH

DRG Contact: Morgan Holmes (COR/L)

MOBIS Task Order	Award Number	Expiration	Performance Period
NORC	AID-OAA-M-13-00013	9/30/2018	N/A
Social Impact*	AID-OAA-M-13-00011	9/30/2018	N/A

PURPOSE:

The Democracy, Human Rights and Governance Learning, Evaluation and Research (DRG-LER) MOBIS task order The DRG Center intends to procure services that will advance learning activities in the DRG foreign assistance sector and provide critical data on the impact of DRG activities in the field to assist with decision making. The new task order is envisioned to support the task of undertaking rigorous evaluations, analyses, and other research within USAID's contracting and program rules and procedures. It will also allow for more substantial involvement and collaboration between the DRG Center staff and academics thus resulting in better learning opportunities and internal USAID staff capacity building.

The objectives of the anticipated mechanism are: (1) to provide U.S. Government and other stakeholders with timely, solid evidence on impact and costs as needed for decision making about DRG foreign assistance intervention expansion and scale up or elimination/scale back; and (2) to contribute to the knowledge base of what works and does not work in the DRG sector. In addition to impact evaluations, the new contract will include performance evaluations, survey research, and qualitative case study research, knowledge dissemination and training; and ancillary studies.

POSSIBLE WORK AREAS:

The primary services & activities to be provided under the task order are:
- Impact evaluations
- Cost Analyses
- Systematic reviews
- Performance evaluations
- Democracy survey research
- Qualitative research, analytical papers and ancillary studies
- Knowledge Dissemination Activities, Workshop and Technical Training

USAID POC:
Morgan Holmes, Tel. 202-712-0175, moholmes@usaid.gov

MOBIS Holder (Large):
NORC
Jeff Telgarsky, Executive Vice President of Research
NORC at the University of Chicago
4350 East-West Highway, 8th Floor, Bethesda MD 20814

MOBIS Holder (Small):
Social Impact
Daniel Sabet, PhD
Social Impact, Inc.
2300 Clarendon Boulevard, Suite 1000

CIVIL SOCIETY AND MEDIA
Increased development of a politically active civil society and a better informed political system (Program Area 2.4)

It is through the advocacy efforts of civil society organizations and civic education that people are empowered to exercise their rights and gain a voice in the process of formulating public policy and political processes. Organizations such as human rights groups, professional associations, religious institutions, pro-democracy groups, environmental activist organizations, business associations, labor unions, media organizations, and think tanks play a vital role in educating and engaging with the public and the government on important local and national issues. Many Civil Society Organizations (CSOs) supported by USAID champion women's rights, ferret out government corruption and impunity, and spotlight business practices that are exploitative of labor and the environment. Their presence and activities of CSOs help assure that government and citizens comply with the rule of law.

Priority Areas: Strengthening the mediums through which citizens can freely organize and communicate with their government and with each other, particularly via support for independent media, democratic labor movements, and the enabling environment for civil society organizations, strengthening a democratic political culture through support for civic engagement and civic education. Through these avenues of support, USAID helps to mobilize constituencies for democratic reform.

Mechanisms and Awards:

GCSS
Global Labor Program
LEEP II
CSOSI

GLOBAL CIVIL SOCIETY STRENGTHENING (GCSS) COOPERATIVE AGREEMENT

DRG Contact: Patricia Hunter (AOR), Tel 202-216-3534, phunter@usaid.gov

Cooperative Agreement	Award Number	Expiration	Performance Period
Counterpart International	DFD-A-00-09-00141-00	09/30/2015	09/30/2020

PURPOSE:
This Leader With Associates consortium will provide technical assistance, design, implementation and evaluation services in support of civil society programming in presence and non-presence countries as identified by USAID Missions and USAID/Washington. USAID-funded assistance mechanisms are frequently called upon in times of crisis, conflict or post-conflict, or when unforeseen challenges or opportunities arise. Such programming is expected to include similar types of activities as those required for the DRG core program in the Leader Award.

GCSS LEADER: The GCSS Leader Award allows USAID DRG and the US Department of State to enhance their global capacity to contribute to more effective civil society strengthening, collaborating with Counterpart International to: design and implement civil society sector assessments; evaluate ongoing USAID programs; conduct research updating USAID's DRG documents; pilot programs to test best practices and new methodologies; and develop training modules and conduct training for development practitioners.

INFORMATION SAFETY AND CAPACITY (ISC) PROJECT. This program will involve a coordinated mix of targeted technical assistance, grants, off-shore web-hosting, deployments of cyber defense and crisis systems, and information sharing to enable NGOs, citizen activists, bloggers, and media (operating in otherwise restrictive environments) to achieve unmonitored and unfettered access to information. Missions or other USAID offices interested in participating in this program should contact the activity technical advisor and AOR, Joshua Haynes (johaynes@usaid.gov).

POSSIBLE GCSS WORK AREAS:
ENHANCING CIVIC PARTICIPATION through:
- **Establishing legal and regulatory frameworks** that protect and promote civil society and civic participation.
- **Strengthening the capacity of Civil Society Organizations (CSOs)** for policy analysis, advocacy, coalition-building, internal governance, membership representation and services, and engaging in other activities aimed at fostering more peaceful and democratic societies.
- **Increasing citizen participation in policy and decision-making** processes, service delivery, resource allocation, oversight of public institutions and in broader initiatives to create more peaceful, democratic, and pluralistic societies.
- **Strengthening political and civic culture that is supportive of democratic institutions** and processes, active citizen participation, civic virtues (tolerance and gender equality), and other civic skills, attitudes, and behaviors.
- **Developing and strengthening independent and democratic trade/labor unions** and federations to promote international core labor standards.

STRENGTHENING INDEPENDENT MEDIA through:
- **Enhancing the technical and theoretical professional capacity of the media** sector through hands-on training, consulting, and mentoring.
- **Strengthening media legal and regulatory frameworks** to enable the growth of independent media.

- **Building financially sustainable media sectors** through activities that enhance both the economic viability of media enterprises and an overall environment that supports the development of sustainable media.
- **Supporting independent media by strengthening media sector CSOs** and related groups/activities—including but not limited to internet-based networking initiatives and regional initiatives.

USAID PROGRAM DESIGN and LEARNING through:
- **Developing and conducting needs assessments, baseline studies, targeted evaluations**, special studies and other information-gathering activities specifically for the design, monitoring and evaluation of USG-funded programs.
- **Developing and disseminating best practices and lessons learned, testing demonstration and pilot models**, and preparing strategic plans and other short-term programming activities.
- **Disseminating technical materials through publications, internet, public forums** and other related events to improve civil society and the media's understanding of the program area.
- **Augmenting CSO capacities to share information** for better learning, especially through the internet and other electronic mediums; and developing analysis-based training materials and modules for stakeholder and development practitioners.

And integrating **CROSS CUTTING THEMES**, such as:

Community Mobilization: Strengthening the capacity of civic groups, community based organizations, professional associations and advocacy groups to contribute to an active civil society.

Youth: Implementing programs, partnerships and policies that actively and constructively involve young people, while helping them to develop the knowledge, skills, and attitudes they need to be active and constructive members of society.

Conflict Mitigation and Transformation: Working to avert imminent violence or the escalation of a dispute into a violent encounter by identifying and addressing the root causes and triggers of conflict. Mitigating ongoing violence and addressing its immediate aftermath.

Labor: Serving as a watchdog for labor rights, labor markets, and labor governance, including worker rights; labor migration and trafficking; labor organizations and trade unions, among others.

Media Outreach: Using mass media (newspapers, magazines, radio, television, internet, text messaging and/or other media) to disseminate information about any aspect of civil society development or citizen empowerment.

GRANTEE/LEADER	GCSS Consortium Partners
Ms. Sibel Berzeg Director, GCSS LWA Counterpart International 2345 Crystal Drive, Suite 301 Arlington, VA 22202 Tel: (703) 236-2284 Fax: (703) 412-5035 Email: sibel@counterpart.org	American Bar Association Rule of Law Initiative (ABA-ROLI) Casals and Associates, Inc. Development Training Services Freedom House International Center for Not-for-Profit Law (ICNL) International Foundation for Electoral Systems (IFES) International Labor and Rights Forum (ILRF) International Research & Exchanges Board (IREX) Management Systems International (MSI)
	RESOURCE PARTNERS
	The American University's Center for Global Peace The Carter Center The International Youth Foundation The Wilson Center Youthbuild International

GLOBAL LABOR PROGRAM COOPERATIVE AGREEMENT

DRG Contact: Patricia Hunter (AOR), Tel 202-216-3534, phunter@usaid.gov

Cooperative Agreement	Award Number	Expiration	Performance Period
Solidarity Center	AID-OAA-L-11-00001	1/31/2016	N/A

PURPOSE:

This LWA for the "Global Labor Program: Promoting International Labor Standards, Improving Workers' Access to Justice and Supporting Independent, Democratic Labor Unions and NGOs" (hereafter, "Global Labor Program") was awarded to the Solidarity Center on 1/31/2011. It continues the important work of promoting international labor standards and strengthening democratic labor unions and NGOs, with focus on the following areas: the promotion of labor justice and the rule of law in the labor sector, gender considerations, continuing improvements in the monitoring and evaluation of program results, and the integration of program objectives with USAID's regional and country-specific development goals.

POSSIBLE WORK AREAS:

USAID and the Solidarity Center continue to focus their work on increasing the capacity of independent, democratic labor movements worldwide to promote core labor standards, effectively represent their members and improve working conditions and workers' livelihoods. The program also explicitly addresses other cross-sectoral development goals including the development of democratic institutions, broad-based economic growth, and healthy and productive workforces and communities.

The Solidarity Center is the lead organization of the cooperative agreement. The four consortium partners include Rutgers' School of Management and Labor Relations (the Labor Studies & Employment Relations Department); Women in Informal Employment Globalizing and Organizing (WIEGO), a global research and policy network on women and the informal economy housed at Harvard University; the Working for America Institute (WAI); and DRG Metrics. DRG developed this leader-associate award mechanism to provide Missions and other U.S. government agencies with a pre-approved grant vehicle that allows for timely procurement of labor-related awards that fall within the scope of the leader award objectives. After the DRG AOR determines whether a proposed activity fits within the award objectives, the Mission may develop and implement its own independent grant or cooperative agreement with the Solidarity Center. These associate awards are managed by the Mission or Bureau. Awards can be extended for up to five years beyond the life of the leader award.

GRANTEE:

Solidarity Center
Nancy Mills, Executive Director
888 16th Street, NW, Suite 400, Washington, DC 20006
Tel: (202) 974-8383; (202) 974-8344;
Web: www.solidaritycenter.org

NGO LEGAL ENABLING ENVIROMENT PROGRAM COOPERATIVE AGREEMENT (LEEP II)

DRG Contact: Patricia Hunter (AOR) Tel 202-216-3534, phunter@usaid.gov and Joshua Haynes (Alternate AOR) 202-712-0836, johaynes@usaid.gov

Cooperative Agreement	Award Number	Expiration	Performance Period
International Center for Not-for-Profit Law	AID-OAA-A-13-00034	08/31/2018	N/A

PURPOSE:

In September 2013, DCHA/DRG/CSM launched the NGO Legal Enabling Environment Program II (LEEP II), a five-year cooperative agreement implemented by the International Center for Not-for-Profit Law (ICNL). The program's main goal is to support and defend freedom of association and assembly for civil society organizations (CSOs) worldwide. This $3.5M program is a five year program that builds on the successes and lessons learned from LEEP I.

LEEP's MAIN PURPOSE, OBJECTIVES AND TYPES OF SUPPORT:

LEEP's main purpose is to support an enabling legal and regulatory environment that protects and promotes civil society and civic participation (Program Element 2.4.1). The program's objectives are:

1) *Technical Assistance:* LEEP II will provide technical assistance to respond to either legislation that threatens civil society and/or to opportunities for enabling civil society reform. The assistance program is designed to be flexible, enabling ICNL to respond rapidly as needs emerge, and supporting longer-term more sustained engagement where necessary and appropriate. The geographic reach of ICNL assistance will be global, with engagements targeting countries in every region, including Africa, Asia, Europe & Eurasia, Latin America & the Caribbean, and the Middle East.

2) *Local Capacity strengthening to advance civil society legal reform:* LEEP II will strengthen local capacity to advance civil society reform through competitively awarded participant training for civil society practitioners, lawyers, scholars, and government officials.

3) *Research:* LEEP II will enrich and enhance the knowledge base for civil society law reform at the country and international level.

POSSIBLE WORK AREAS:

- LEEP II offers both in-country and remote technical assistance. Under LEEP II, ICNL works with DCHA/DRG, Regional Bureaus, and Missions to develop appropriate annual work plans that identify and prioritize countries for technical assistance.
- LEEP II can also provide rapid response technical assistance for a small number of urgent, high priority situations not envisioned in the work plan. Illustrative activities include written analysis of NGO-related legislation, one to two trips by ICNL staff to conduct an assessment and/or provide technical assistance, and/or provision of a small grant to local partners to help advance NGO law reform.
- LEEP II is intended to provide limited technical assistance when Mission resources are unavailable, or when rapidly evolving situations require an immediate response that precludes normal Mission-based procurement, or when the scope and cost of the activity is so limited as to make Mission funding cumbersome and inefficient. In cases in which a Mission, Bureau, or other USG partner requests urgent assistance to undertake an activity more expansive than the limited interventions covered by LEEP II or in excess of the DG funding available for LEEP II activities, DRG may be able to accommodate the activity when the party requesting the assistance agrees to transfer the funds to the core agreement. In all cases in which more extensive interventions are required, the Mission is encouraged to directly fund that assistance. DRG/CSM is available to offer guidance to Missions as needed.

CONTACT INFORMATION:

International Center for Not-for-Profit Law (ICNL)
Douglas Rutzen and David Moore

1126 16th Street, NW, Suite 400
Washington, DC 20036
Tel: (202) 452-8600
Fax: (202) 452-8555
E-mail: drutzen@icnl.org; david@icnl.org.hu
Web: www.icnl.org

CIVIL SOCIETY ORGANIZATION SUSTAINABILITY INDEX (CSOSI)

DRG Contact: Maryanne Yerkes (COR) Tel. 202-712-0915, myerkes@usaid.gov

IQC Task Order	Order Number	Expiration	Performance Period
Management Systems International	AID-OAA-TO-11-00036	6/17/2016	N/A

PURPOSE:

In October 2010, DRG, AFR/SD, and an external resource partner introduced the NGO Sustainability Index for Sub-Saharan Africa (NGOSI), an analytical tool for measuring the sustainability of NGOs, in 19 Sub-Saharan African countries. This was followed in 2011 by the introduction of the tool to the Middle East and North Africa (MENA) region. The purpose is to provide users with a way to assess the sustainability of the civil society sector in a given country as well as a way to identify and compare the trends and issues affecting NGOs across the region and to enable comparisons to be drawn between Africa, the Middle-East, Europe, and Eurasia.

The NGOSI offers:

- a management tool for monitoring, measuring, and evaluating progress in sectoral development;
- a way to focus resources and efforts on critical areas of civil society reform;
- a guide to the challenges and opportunities facing NGOs and civil society generally;
- a set of qualitative indicators in a user-friendly quantitative form; and,
- narrative country reports prepared by local NGOs.

To view the NGOSI for Sub-Saharan Africa and for Europe and Eurasia, visit: E&E – http://www.usaid.gov/locations/europe_eurasia/dem_gov/ngoindex/ , and AFR – http://www.usaid.gov/our_work/democracy_and_governance/technical_areas/civil_society/angosi/.

POSSIBLE WORK AREAS: The NGOSI for Sub-Saharan Africa and for MENA, which are modeled on the NGOSI for Central and Eastern Europe and Eurasia, measures NGO sustainability using a methodology that employs seven indicators or "dimensions." These dimensions include legal environment; organizational capacity; financial viability; advocacy; service provision; infrastructure; and, public image. Each dimension is rated along a seven-point scale with 1 indicating an advanced level of development and 7 indicating a low level. Mid-range scores between 3.1 and 5 indicate an evolving level.

By combining numerical scores with narrative explanations, the Index provides a foundation, or baseline, for identifying the challenges and opportunities facing the selected countries. As countries are grouped by sub-region, users can track sub-regional differences, the impact of internal and external factors, as well as the relationship between NGO sustainability and other development trends. In addition, the NGOSI contains thematic essays that highlight regional trends and issues. By drawing on the NGOSI, users will be better able to determine priorities and approaches.

Missions and Regional Bureaus who may be interested in having the NGOSI in their region or country are welcome to contact the COR to discuss possible expansion into your country or region. Through a resource partnership, the NGOSI will be launched in Afghanistan and Pakistan in 2011.

CONTACT INFORMATION:

Management Systems International
Lisa Slifer-Mbacke, Technical Director
Washington, DC
Tel: (202) 484-7170 x. 664, E-mail: lslifermbacke@msi-inc.com

ELECTIONS AND POLITICAL TRANSITIONS
More genuine and competitive political processes
(Program Area 2.3)

Elections can be a primary tool to help force political openings and expand political participation. The electoral process has often been a principal vehicle for democratization, as authoritarian governments have frequently fallen to democratic forces. For an election to be free and fair, certain civil liberties, such as the freedoms of speech, association, and assembly are required. Elections offer political parties and civic groups an opportunity to mobilize and organize supporters and share alternative platforms with the public. Electoral campaigns also tend to foster political liberalization. They also serve to encourage political debate.

Priority Areas: Impartial electoral frameworks, credible electoral administration, effective oversight of electoral processes, informed and active citizenries, representative and competitive multi-party systems, inclusion of women and other disadvantaged groups, effective governance by elected leaders and bodies, election monitoring, voter education and effective transfers of political power.

Mechanisms and Funds:

CEPPS III
EPP Fund

CONSORTIUM FOR ELECTIONS AND POLITICAL PROCESSES STRENGTHENING III (CEPPS III)

DRG Contact: Tess McEnery (AOR) Tel 202-712-0658, tmcenery@usaid.gov and Jeffrey Vanness (Alternate AOR) Tel 202-712-4516, jvanness@usaid.gov

Cooperative Agreement	Award Number	Expiration	Performance Period
CEPPS III	DFD-A-00-08-00350-00	9/29/2014	9/29/2019

PURPOSE:

In 2008, DRG awarded a Leader With Associates (LWA) cooperative agreement to the Consortium for Elections and Political Process Strengthening (CEPPS): a joint venture between the International Foundation for Electoral Systems (IFES), the International Republican Institute (IRI), and the National Democratic Institute for International Affairs (NDI). All three organizations are leaders in the field of elections and political processes and possess a vast amount of experience and expertise. CEPPS III programs may be implemented by one member of the consortium, by two or more working on activities separately, or by two or more members working jointly.

The purpose of this agreement is to strengthen and support democratic electoral and political processes by providing access to a full array of activities in the field of elections and political processes. The emphasis is on long-term planning and sustainable development of electoral and political processes rather than event-driven, crisis-oriented activities centered on a single election. The award was designed to allow for the initiation and implementation of short- and long-term activities without requiring a time-consuming competitive application process.

POSSIBLE WORK AREAS:

The CEPPS III Leader With Associates Cooperative Agreement is designed to respond to immediate and long-term Mission and bureau needs related to assessments, strategy formulation, activity design, evaluation, and program implementation. Activities initiated under this award may promote any of the following ten objectives:

Objective 1: Impartial Legal Framework for Elections and Political Parties

Although not a sufficient condition in isolation, an impartial framework (i.e. constitutional provisions, laws, rules, regulations, and institutions which govern electoral and political processes) is a necessary condition for sustainable, credible electoral processes and representative, democratic political parties.

Objective 2: Credible Electoral Administration

Credible electoral administration requires an impartial, transparent, and competent electoral authority managing the elections, and sufficient resources to permit neutral administration. It also requires professional staff who are competent in key areas of electoral administration, including registration, designating polling sites, drawing up voters' lists, tabulating votes, providing security, enforcing political finance rules, using computer hardware and software effectively, educating voters and adjudicating complaints if within the electoral authority's mandate.

Objective 3: An Informed and Active Citizenry

An informed and active citizenry is the driving force behind a genuine and competitive political process. It also helps build confidence in the system, and public acceptance of results. Free and fair elections require that all citizens understand the electoral system and political choices, and participate in political processes through party membership, voting, volunteer service, and membership in NGOs.

Objective 4: Effective Oversight of Electoral Processes

Monitoring electoral processes can reduce the opportunities and incentives for electoral fraud, identify shortcomings of the electoral process with the intention of facilitating genuine and competitive elections, and legitimize a peaceful transfer of power. Recognizing that election day comprises only one component of the electoral process, effective oversight of electoral processes includes sufficient pre/post-election monitoring. Election monitors may include: political contestants who monitor violations of their supporters' political rights, nonpartisan citizen organizations, and international organizations which evaluate a country's electoral framework and administration compared to international standards and practices. The media can also serve a useful watchdog function during an electoral process if it has the capacity to produce credible and accurate reports about the preparations for, and the conduct of, elections. Monitoring of the electoral process -- by international organizations, domestic monitors, political party poll watchers or local media -- can lend confidence in the outcome of an election.

Objective 5: Increased Political Participation of Women, Persons with Disabilities, and Other Historically Disenfranchised Groups

This objective promotes increased political participation of groups that have historically been excluded from fair participation. Illustrative examples of these groups include (but are not limited to) women, minorities, internally displaced persons (IDPs), and persons with disabilities. To ensure the inclusion of these groups, and others, in electoral activities, it is critical that electoral laws, administration and oversight are non-discriminatory and non-exclusionary, and that civil and political rights of politically marginalized groups are protected through effective enforcement. This objective aims not only to remove barriers to participation, but also to improve political participation and representation through targeted training, skills development and effective voter education. The goal is to strengthen the capacity of historically disenfranchised groups to participate in and influence decision-making bodies within political parties and government.

Objective 6: Consensus-building to promote peaceful agreement on democratic reform

This objective aims to develop processes for promoting peaceful agreement for democratic reform through broad-based participation in determining and negotiating changes to governing structures.

Objective 7: Representative and Competitive Multiparty System

A representative and competitive multiparty system consists of political parties which have internal democratic procedures, and broader institutional structures that are accountable, transparent, inclusive of sub-populations, and accepted by party members. Representative political parties serve many functions such as acting as intermediaries between the electorate and the elected; involving members of different ethnicities, religious beliefs or genders; developing platforms-based citizen input; and ensuring effective communications between political party structures and constituencies.

Objective 8: Effective Transfer of Political Power

Genuine and competitive political processes require: the peaceful transfer of power between different individuals, groups, or political parties through established procedures; losing parties accepting the outcome of the election and the authority of newly elected officials; and public recognition of the legitimacy of the process. Newly elected officials must be prepared to fulfill their responsibilities, and political parties must be prepared to assume a proper governance role.

Objective 9: Effective Governance by Elected Leaders and Bodies

Elected leaders must be able to govern effectively once they take office. Parties and their leaders at the national, regional and local level need to serve the public, rather than private interests. Legislative bodies need to develop technical skills, as well as rules of procedure and ways of operating which enhance their ability to develop legislation and to provide oversight of the executive branch. At the local level, mayors and councils need to be able to work together as well as perform their specific functions such that the local community benefits from democratically elected government.

Objective 10: Promoting Sustainable Local/Regional Organizations Engaged in Election Assistance

USAID aims to strengthen the capacity of indigenous local/regional organizations in developing countries to: 1) conduct elections related activities; and 2) provide technical assistance and training to other local organizations on elections and political processes. The rationale is that *strengthened* election-oriented organizations in developing countries will: 1) broaden the community of democracy promoters and advocates abroad; 2) demonstrate that USAID assistance leads directly to sustainable change among local organizations, without dependence on intermediary organizations; and 3) promote replication.

GRANTEES:

*The Consortium for Elections and Political Processes Strengthening is a joint venture of the following three organizations: International Foundation for Electoral Systems (IFES), International Republican Institute (IRI), and National Democratic Institute for International Affairs (NDI). IRI is the administrative manager for CEPPS and as such, all communication regarding CEPPS should be sent to the office of CEPPS Director, Ms. Sondra Govatski.

CEPPS Administration
c/o International Republican Institute
Sondra Govatski
1225 Eye Street, NW Suite 700
Washington, DC 20005-5962
Tel: (202) 408-9450
Fax: (202) 408-9462
E-mail: sgovatski@iri.org

ELECTIONS AND POLITICAL PROCESSES FUND

DRG Contact: Monica Moore, Fund Manager

PURPOSE:

The purpose of the Elections and Political Processes (EPP) Fund is to provide assistance in cases of critical unanticipated need with regards to electoral and political processes. The Fund is global in reach; since the Fund was established in 2006, $111 million of assistance has been provided to 72 countries.

POSSIBLE WORK AREAS:

All USAID Missions may apply for funding. The EPP Fund solicits applications from USAID Missions for competitive funding rounds each fiscal year. In addition, the EPP Fund accepts ad hoc applications if urgent needs arise outside of funding rounds. Applications are assessed by a cross-Agency review committee. To be successful, applications must meet at least two of the following three criteria:

•   Proposed program addresses snap elections or other unanticipated needs;
•   Proposed program exploits a targeted window of opportunity for EPP Funds and justifies how EPP Funds will fit with existing USG and other donor efforts; and
•   Proposed program is determined to be unique and innovative by the EPP Fund review committee.

EPP Fund applications must be submitted through an online application system:
http://dg.usaidallnet.gov/dgepp/login.php

EPP Fund projects cover a wide range of activities. Some areas that have been addressed include: Post-conflict peace and constitutional design processes; political violence, electoral violence and political instability; urgent needs created by snap elections; citizen oversight of elections; protection and promotion of democratic governance in backsliding countries; and other electoral and broader political processes in priority countries.

CONTACT INFORMATION:

Monica Moore
Fund Manager
Tel: (202) 712-0771
Fax: (202) 204-3042
E-mail: momoore@usaid.gov
Web: http://dg.usaidallnet.gov/dgepp/login.php

GOVERNANCE
More transparent and accountable government institutions (Program Area 2.2)

Many citizens of developing countries recognize the intrinsic value of democratic principles and processes (e.g., elections, human rights, and representation). At the same time, they are concerned with a government's ability to function. In general, governance issues pertain to the ability of government to develop an efficient and effective public management process. Because citizens lose confidence in a government that is unable to meet their basic security and service needs, the degree to which a government is able to carry out its responsibilities at any level is often a key determinant of a country's ability to sustain democratic reform.

Priority Areas: Legislative strengthening, public policy development and implementation, decentralization and local capacity, anticorruption initiatives, and security sector reform.

Mechanisms:

Legislative Strengthening Technical Services IQC

AND

RULE OF LAW
Strengthening rule of law (Program Area 2.1)

The rule of law (RoL) sector is viewed through the prism of the DRG analytic framework: The Rule of Law Strategic Framework. Using this framework helps in systematically identifying the problems and weaknesses with rule of law in a country and suggests a range of potential programmatic approaches to problems in the rule of law. The DRG Center helps Missions undertake strategic analyses that link building rule of law with strengthening democracy. It supports efforts to strengthen five elements comprising the rule of law: Order and security; Legitimacy; Checks and balances; Fairness (Equal application of the law; Procedural fairness; Protection of human rights and civil liberties; and Access to justice); and Effective application.

Mechanisms:

ENGAGE IQC
ROL IQC
The Rights Consortium

LEGISLATIVE STRENGTHENING TECHNICAL SERVICES IQCS

DRG Contact: Keith Schulz (COR, GROL)   Tel. 202-712-4219; keschulz@usaid.gov

IQCs	Award Number	Expiration	Performance Period
Tetra Tech ARD	AID-OAA-I-12-00001	11/9/2016	11/9/2019
Chemonics International	AID-OAA-I-12-00002	11/9/2016	11/9/2019
DAI	AID-OAA-I-12-00003	11/9/2016	11/9/2019
Social Impact, Inc.	AID-OAA-I-12-00004	11/9/2016	11/9/2019
SUNY/CID	AID-OAA-I-12-00005	11/9/2016	11/9/2019

PURPOSE:

The purpose of this contract is to improve the capacity and performance of legislatures, their members, and staff in realizing their representative, lawmaking, and oversight functions. This activity establishes a mechanism for missions to assist national, provincial and municipal legislative or representative bodies improve their deliberative processes so that they are more democratic, transparent, accountable, and effective, better represent the public interest, and result in better monitoring of governmental performance. The IQC enables a holistic approach to legislative strengthening and includes possible support to a broad spectrum of stakeholders who have an interest in the functioning and activities of the legislature including legislative members & staff, other government actors, civil society, political parties, media, and private sector.

POSSIBLE WORK AREAS:

The contractor may be called upon to provide advice, assistance and training for legislative members and staff, host country officials, and civil society representatives on the development of democratic legislative practice and procedures including, but not limited to, the following areas:

Representation
- Improving links between legislators to their constituencies and subnational government bodies by supporting best practices in areas such as constituency outreach, policy dialogue, public meetings/hearings, and public policy mediation/negotiation;
- Enhancing support for the legislature through activities designed to increase public participation in the legislative process, improve civil society advocacy, promote more professional media coverage of legislative issues, and increase the quality of policy analysis, information, and research available to the legislature.

Lawmaking
- Strengthening analytical skills to enable critical review of draft legislation and more evidence-based legislation;
- Providing advisory services on the drafting, enforcement and implementation of laws and regulations;
- Improving legislative committee operations and effectiveness as well as legislative support services in areas such as research, budget analysis, public outreach and communications, and ICT;
- Working to strengthen political groups, factions and caucuses including on responsibility of majority parties and coalitions, constructive opposition, developing legislative and policy agendas and public outreach;

Oversight
- Providing assistance and training on budget formulation, review and oversight;
- Strengthening accountability mechanisms for policy review and enforcement;
- Supporting civil society efforts to monitor and oversee the work of deliberative bodies:

Public Administration
- Building institutional capacity in strategic planning, human resources, financial management and general public administration;

Research

- Conducting legislative assessements, designing strategies and evaluating legislative assistance programs;
- Conducting research and advancing knowledge on topics relevant to legislative strengthening;

Cross cutting Support for Donor Programs
- Supporting USAID, host government and donor sectoral programs and initiatives (such as health, education, economic growth, and environment) through support to policy reform, budget formulation, and oversight;
- Assisting USAID procurement reform and use of host country systems through strengthening of budget oversight and government accountability

CONTRACTORS

Tetra Tech ARD, Inc.	Chemonics International	Social Impact*
Jessie Biddle (Sr. Legislative Advisor) (IQC Manager) 159 Bank St., Suite 300 Burlington, VT 05401-1397 Tel: (802) 658-3890 Fax: (802) 658-4247 Email: ard@ardinc.com jesse.biddle@tetratech.com david.green@tetratech.com Web: www.ardinc.com Subcontractors: Parliamentary Center, Canada; Development and Training Services, Inc. (dTS); The Graduate School's International Institute; IREX; World Learning	Maggie Seminario (Sr. Legislative Advisor) Lisa Dickieson (IQC Manager) 1717 H Street, NW Washington, DC 20006 Tel: (202) 955-3300 Fax: (202) 955-3400 Email: mseminario@chemonics.com ldickieson@chemonics.com Web: www.chemonics.com Subcontractors: Urban Institute; Partners for Democratic Change; Center for Democracy and Election Management at American University; Public Law Center, Loyola and Tulane Universities; State Legislative Leaders Foundation; LTL Strategies	Gary Bland – RTI International (Sr. Legislative Advisor) Andrew Green – Social Impact (IQC Manager) 2300 Clarendon Blvd, Suite 300 Arlington, VA 22201 Tel: (703) 465-1884 Fax: (703) 465-1888 Email: agreen@socialimpact.com gbland@rti.org Web: www.socialimpact.com Subcontractors: RTI International; Ohio State University; Global Partners and Associates; Women's Campaign International; National Center for State Courts (NCSC); HGM Management and Technologies, Inc.
Development Alternatives Inc. (DAI) Carmen Lane (Sr. Legislative Advisor) Jeremy Kanthor (IQC Manager) 7600 Wisconsin Avenue, Suite 200 Bethesda, MD. 20814 Tel: (301) 771-7600 Fax: (301) 771-7777 Email: Contracts@dai.com carmen_lane@dai.com Jeremy_kanthor@dai.com Web: www.dai.com Subcontractors: National Conference of State Legislatures (NCSL); International Consortium for Law and Development (ICLAD); Internews; Charney Research; Alpha XP Web Software, LLC; Mosley & Associates	**The Research Foundation of the State University of New York, Center for International Development (SUNY/CID)** Robert Nakamura (Sr. Legislative Advisor) Cecelia Skott (IQC Manager) 1400 Washington Avenue –MSC 312 Albany, NY 12222 Fax: (518) 443-5124 Email: rnakamura@albany.edu cskott@albany.edu Web: http://www.cid.suny.edu/ Subcontractors: Management Systems International (MSI); Amex International, Inc; Blue Law International, LLP; The Asia Foundation (TAF); United States Association of Former Members of Congress (USAFMC)	

*This is a small business.

IQCS FOR ENCOURAGING GLOBAL ANTICORRUPTION AND GOOD GOVERNANCE (ENGAGE)

DRG Contact: Kenneth Barden (COR, GROL) Tel 202-712-0527, kbarden@usaid.gov, Keith Schulz (Alternate, GROL) Tel 202-712-4219; keschulz@usaid.gov

IQCs	Award Number	Expiration Date	Performance Period
Tetra Tech ARD, Inc.	DFD-I-00-08-00067-00	3/13/2015	3/13/2016
Casals and Associates, Inc.	DFD-I-00-08-00069-00	3/13/2015	3/13/2016
Chemonics International Inc.	DFD-I-00-08-00070-00	3/13/2015	3/13/2016
Development Alternatives Inc.	DFD-I-00-08-00071-00	3/13/2015	3/13/2016
Management Systems International, Inc. (MSI)	DFD-I-00-08-00072-00	3/13/2015	3/13/2016
QED Group, LLC (QED) *	DFD-I-00-08-00073-00	3/13/2015	3/13/2016

* This is a small business.

PURPOSE:

The connections between public sector corruption and development run deep. Some of them are clear and direct, for instance when political officials divert aid and investment capital to offshore bank accounts, poor nations become poorer. When political, bureaucratic, and judicial processes are put up for rent, it endangers civil liberties and property rights. Corruption erodes the quality of public services and access to those services. Political and economic benefits flow to a limited number of individuals, while the costs are extracted from society at large -- often from the poor and powerless. While the tangible and immediate damage can be significant, other detrimental impacts are intangible, collective, and long-term in nature. Corruption can erode the legitimacy of government and undermine democratic values like trust, tolerance, accountability, and participation. Corruption can increase the time, cost, and uncertainty of doing business and thereby deter investment, or skew investment toward high-return sectors or white elephant projects whose main beneficiaries are contract winners and those who receive kickbacks, not the public as a whole. Corruption can also reduce competition, lower compliance with construction, environmental, or other regulations, increase budgetary pressures on government, and nourish organized crime networks.

The objective of ENGAGE is to provide USAID and its partner countries with the broad range of technical assistance, assessments and other resources necessary to develop and implement appropriate and meaningful strategies to curb corruption in economic, political and social service sectors. USAID defines corruption as "the abuse of entrusted authority for private gain." Thus, the activities under ENGAGE address unilateral abuses by governmental officials such as embezzlement and nepotism, as well as abuses linking public and private actors such as bribery, extortion, influence peddling, and fraud at both lower and higher levels of government and the public sector (i.e., "administrative" and "grand" corruption). The activities under this IQC address three broad areas: 1) public financial, administrative and regulatory measures that promote transparency, accountability and effective governance; 2) civil society advocacy on behalf of governmental integrity, implementation of anticorruption programs and/or oversight of public functions and authorities; and 3) incorporation of anticorruption promotion into other sectoral/sub-sectoral areas, such as health and education, natural resource management, corporate governance, or into key aspects of democracy promotion, such as rule of law, legislative oversight or local government strengthening.

POSSIBLE WORK AREAS

Activities may be carried out with regard to a given sector (e.g., democracy and governance, health, environment, education, economic growth), or across several sectors. The list of possible activities is indicative, not necessarily exhaustive.

- Public administration reform
- Administrative and legal sanction regimes
- E-Government reform
- Transparent budget making and implementation
- Procurement reform
- Financial management systems
- Audit institutions and internal control regimes
- Government ethics regimes
- Regulatory reform
- Tax and customs administration
- Inspector General/Ombudsmen/Anticorruption Agencies
- Complaint mechanisms and whistle-blower protections
- Legislative oversight
- Anticorruption legislation (e.g. criminalization of bribery, FOIA, etc.) & other relevant legal frameworks
- Justice sector reform
- Decentralization and transparency in local government
- Political finance reform and regulation
- Oversight and transparency regimes for electoral commissions
- Financial disclosure regimes
- Transparent privatization processes
- Procurement reform
- Tax and customs collections
- Corporate governance and codes of ethics
- Extractive industry transparency
- Financial disclosure and conflict of interest regimes
- Civil society advocacy, anticorruption programming and oversight of government (organizational development, advocacy and oversight strategies, coalition building, managing relations with government)
- Open budget processes and budget oversight
- Freedom of information legislation and access to information
- Investigative journalism and other media strengthening
- Public education campaigns
- Corruption surveys, user surveys and report cards and dissemination of results
- Local government transparency
- Participatory budgeting
- Community oversight of service delivery
- The development and dissemination of anticorruption strategies, activities and lessons learned
- Programs to address corruption in public service delivery
- Public-private partnerships to combat corruption
- Survey techniques and corruption measurement
- Measurement and evaluation of anticorruption impact
- Approaches designed specifically to address the challenge of corruption in fragile states and reconstruction settings

PRIME CONTRACTORS		
Tetra Tech ARD, Inc. Aaron Chassy and Don Bowser 159 Bank Street, Suite 300 Burlington, VT 05401 Tel: (802) 658-3890 Email: achassy@ardinc.com Web: www.tetratechintdev.com/	**Casals and Associates Inc.** Michael Geertson and David Cohen 1199 North Fairfax Street, 3rd Floor Alexandria, VA 22314 Tel: (703) 920-5750 Email: mgeertson@casals.com ; dcohen@casals.com Web: www.casals.com	**Chemonics International Inc.** Michelle Drayer and Saroeun Earm 1717 H Street NW Washington, DC 20036 Tel: (202) 955-3300 Email: mdrayer@chemonics.com; searm@chemonics.com Web: www.chemonics.com
Development Alternatives, Inc. Jeremy Kanthor and Marianne Camerer 7600 Wisconsin Avenue, Suite 200 Bethesda, MD 20814 Tel: (301) 771-7600 Fax: (301) 771-7777 Email: jeremy_kanthor@dai.com Web: www.dai.com	**Management Systems International** Stacy Stacks and Bert Spector 600 Water Street, SW Washington, DC 20024-4288 Tel: (202) 484-7170 Email: sstacks@msi-inc.com; bspector@msi-inc.com Web: www.msiworldwide.com	**The QED Group, LLC** Larry Birch and Keith Henderson 1250 Eye Street NW, Suite 1100 Washington, DC 20005 Tel: (202) 521-1919 Web: www.qedgroupllc.com
SUB CONTRACTORS (ICQS)		
To Associates in Rural Development, Inc.: Bankworld Inc. BearingPoint, Inc. Contracting Assessment Researches (CAR) Cooperative League of the USA (CLUSA) Development & Training Services, Inc. (dTS) Diane Cromer Enterprises Financial Services Volunteer Corps (FSVC) Humphreys Consulting, LLC Institutional Reform and the Informal Sector (The IRIS Center) International Research & Exchanges Board (IREX) MetaMetrics Inc. World Learning for International Development	**To Casals and Associates, Inc.:** AMIDEST The Asia Foundation (TAF) Boston University Claro & Associates, Inc. Commonwealth Trading Partners EAM, Inc./Mosley & Associates EDF Consulting, Inc. The Emergency Group, Ltd. Enterprise Solutions, Inc. Eurasia Foundation International Decision Strategies, Inc. International Foundation for Electoral Systems (IFES) Mendez England & Associates, Pact International UHY Advisors Vanderbilt University World Resources Institute (WRI)	**To Chemonics International Inc.:** Alfa XP Web Software Company, LLC. BlueForce International, LLC. Electoral Reform International Services Ltd. Institute for Sustainable Communities QED Group, LLC. The Urban Institute

To Development Alternatives Inc.:	To Management Systems International, Inc.:	To QED Group, LLC (QED) (Small Business Set-aside):
Computer Frontiers	American Institutes for Research	Academy for Educational Development
East-West Management Institute	Camris International, Inc.	The Borders Group
Global Business Solutions	Center for International Private Enterprise	Comptrollers and Treasurers
Global Integrity	Checchi and Company Consulting, Inc.	East-West Management Institute
Innovative Resources Management	Emerging Market Group, Ltd.	Institute for Public-Private Partnerships
Internews Network	The Gallup Organization	International Law Institute
Jacobs & Associates	Heartlands International, Ltd.	International City/County Management Association
Michael Borish & Company	International Center for Journalists,	International Research and Exchange Board
Social Impact	International Development Business Consultants, LLC,	Millennium International Consulting
Zogby International	International Organization for Migration	National Association of State Auditors
	JE Austin Associates, Inc.	National Judicial College
	PA Government Services Inc.	Partners for Democratic Change
	Partners of the Americas	Spearman, Welch & Associates
	Police Foundation	WISeKey USA, Inc.
	SEGURA Consulting, LLC.	
	University Research Company, LLC.	
	Voxina, Inc.	

KEY SUBCONTRACTOR (PILOT):

These IQCs are part of a Key Subcontractor Pilot introduced by the Office of Acquisition and Assistance. Prior to issuing any task order under these IQCs, Contracting Officers/Negotiators must address the Key Subcontractors provision in Section H.21 Some contractors did not propose any Key Subcontractors and therefore are exempt from this requirement.

IQCS FOR RULE OF LAW

DRG Contacts: Keith Crawford, kcrawford@usaid.gov (COR, GROL); Achieng Akumu, aakumu@usaid.gov (Alternate COR, GROL)

IQCs	Award Number	Expiration Date	Performance Period
AMEX*	AID-OAA-I-13-00024	2/7/2018	2/7/2019
Casals & Associates	AID-OAA-I-13-00039	2/7/2018	2/7/2019
Checchi Consulting	AID-OAA-I-13-00044	2/7/2018	2/7/2019
Chemonics International Inc.	AID-OAA-I-13-00032	2/7/2018	2/7/2019
Development Alternatives Inc.	AID-OAA-I-13-00033	2/7/2018	2/7/2019
Democracy International*	AID-OAA-I-13-00030	2/7/2018	2/7/2019
East-West Management Institute	AID-OAA-I-13-00033	2/7/2018	2/7/2019
Millennium DPI*	AID-OAA-I-13-00029	2/7/2018	2/7/2019
Tetra Tech DPK	AID-OAA-I-13-00036	2/7/2018	2/7/2019

* This is a small business.

PURPOSE: The Rule of Law (ROL) IQC mechanism is vital to supporting the foreign assistance objective of Governing Justly and Democratically – to promote and strengthen effective democracies in recipient states and move them along a continuum toward democratic consolidation. The ROL IQC provides the Center of Excellence on Democracy, Human Rights and Governance in the Bureau of Democracy, Conflict and Humanitarian Assistance (DCHA/DRG) invaluable support to serve missions' programs in the area of new or ongoing legal reform assistance initiatives.

POSSIBLE WORK AREAS

This IQC will entail the provision of a wide array of support services encompassing short- and long-term technical assistance and other activities aimed at supporting the development of rule of law and human rights. The IQC will be managed by USAID staff. However, cooperating U.S. Agencies, such as the Department of State and the Millennium Challenge Corporation, may opt to transfer funds to USAID in order to participate in shared programs. Activities will support a broad range of governmental and non-governmental actors to advance the following objectives toward advancing the rule of law:

- Order and Security
- Legitimate Constitutions, Laws and Legal Institutions
- Strengthened Checks and Balances
- Fairness and Human Rights
- Effective Application of the Law
- Rule of law in post-conflict environments

Tasks and Deliverables: The contractor shall provide the following tasks/deliverables as requested in task orders under this contract to accomplish the objectives:

- Conducting rule of law assessments, evaluations, developing strategies, and designing programs. This also includes justice sector institutional analysis, planning, and diagnostic surveys;
- Legal analysis and research (in common and civil law systems, comparative legal systems, customary, religious or traditional or religious legal systems, international law, labor law, constitutional law, business law, commercial law, law of associations, administrative law, and general law);

- Assisting in the development of strategies, programs, and activities that optimize linkages between the justice sector institutions and other sector areas;
- Advising government officials and/or USAID on the best practices to strengthen the justice sector, advance human rights, and support cooperation among government institutions;
- Advising governments and/or USAID on how to develop and implement justice sector activities;
- Supporting, through provision of staff, technical services and/or material support, start-up and/or longer-term implementation of justice sector initiatives;
- Judicial, legal, human rights and other justice sector training;
- Supporting the establishment of judicial or legal training institutes, law schools, legal education, continuing legal education, curriculum development, and judicial system strengthening programs;
- Training to host country officials on oversight, ethics, conflict of interest, and rule of law related functions;
- Providing advisory services pertaining to drafting and enforcement of regulations and laws;
- Supporting capacity building initiatives and/or providing grants to governmental or civil society organizations (CSOs) for advocacy and monitoring, professional associations, strategic planning, legal aid clinics, organization, funding or other needs;
- Capacity building to develop holistic programs for victims of violence and crime including crime prevention, treatment, investigation, prosecution, and referral;
- Facilitating mechanisms for public participation in legal reform and policy decision-making;
- Facilitating government inter-institutional coordination mechanisms of the justice sector;
- Sponsoring investigative journalism training and other related monitoring activities of the justice sector;
- Training, research and analysis on cross-sectoral and emerging issues, e.g., corruption, economic growth, gender-based violence, HIV/AIDS discrimination, etc.;
- Research, analysis and publication of lessons learned regarding rule of law challenges, impact, and programming;
- Financial analysis, auditing of justice sector institutions, and Procurement/logistics (e.g., computers and office supplies); and
- Workshop and conference planning, Public outreach, awareness-raising, Publishing documents (e.g., monographs, studies, laws, judicial decisions), and minor rehabilitation of justice sector buildings.

CONTRACTORS		
AMEX	**Democracy International**	**Millennium DPI**
Mori Diané mori@amexdc.com	Glenn Cowan gcowan@democracyinternational.com	Brian Hannon brianhannon@me.com
Jody Schubert jschubert@amexdc.com	Evan Smith esmith@democracyinternational.com	Esther Wilson Hannon ewhannon@millenniumpartners.org
Fota Ishaq fishaq@amexdc.com	Eric Bjornlund eric@democracyinternational.com	Natalija Stamenkovic n.stamenkovic@developmentpi.com

Casals & Associates	Checchi Consulting	Chemonics International Inc.
Jeanine Zeitvogel, Vice President jeanine.zeitvogel@dyn-intl.com Charles Harvey, Senior Contracts Manager charles.harvey@dyn-intl.com	James Agee jagee@checchiconsulting.com Ruslan Konstantinov rkonstantinov@checchiconsulting.com Patricia McPhelim pmcphelim@checchiconsulting.com	Christopher Scott cscott@chemonics.com Lisa Dickieson ldickieson@chemonics.com Deborah Perlman dperlman@chemonics.com
Development Alternatives Inc. (DAI) Gregory Gisvold greg_gisvold@dai.com Baigal Darambazar baigal_darambazar@dai.com	East-West Management Institute Adrian Hewryk ahewryk@ewmi.org Rachel Tritt rtritt@ewmi.org	Tetra Tech DPK Jason Schwarz jschwarz@dpkconsulting.com Mark Johnson Mark.Johnson@tetratech.com Crystal Costa ccosta@dpkconsulting.com Robert Page rpage@dpkconsulting.com

HUMAN RIGHTS AND RULE OF LAW COOPERATIVE AGREEMENT/ RIGHTS CONSORTIUM

DRG Contact: Keith Crawford (AOR, GROL) kcrawford@usaid.gov and Achieng Akumu (Alternate AOR, GROL) aakumu@usaid.gov

Cooperative Agreement	Award Number	Expiration	Period of Performance
RIGHTS Consortium	DFD-A-A-00-09-00058-00	10/11/2014	10/11/2019

PURPOSE:

DRG has awarded a Leader With Associates (LWA) cooperative agreement to Freedom House on behalf of the Rights Consortium. The RIGHTS Consortium brings together the formidable capabilities and geographical and substantive reach of three primary partners, Freedom House, the American Bar Association's Rule of Law Initiative, and the National Democratic Institute for International Affairs.

Reflective of the need to cover the full range of rule of law challenges, the RIGHTS Consortium also includes associate partners who will also contribute their expertise in specific areas: The Center for the Administration of Justice at Florida International University (in the areas of police and justice sector reform), The Texas Regional Center for Policing Innovation at Sam Houston State University (police training on community policing), Global Rights (for reaching vulnerable populations in conflict and post-conflict environments), The Carter Center (for conflict mitigation and resolution in divided societies), The International Center for Not-for-Profit Law (for promotion and defense of civil society through legal frameworks); The Center for Victims of Torture (on issues of torture and strategic and tactical planning for reform); and The American Center for International Labor Solidarity (for labor laws, practice, and dispute mechanisms in line with international standards).

Together, they will enhance the Agency's capacity to promote respect for human rights and the rule of law by providing access to NGOs with extensive human rights and rule of law expertise. Activities may aim to reform legal frameworks and/or strengthen actors and institutions within and beyond the justice sector, including but not limited to the judiciary, prosecutors, legal defense, investigators, civilian police, traditional authorities, civil society, and citizens.

POSSIBLE WORK AREAS:

As viewed through the prism of the DRG Rule of Law Strategic Framework, the Rights Consortium offers programs in the following areas:

1. Order and Security: Improving capacity to protect persons, property, and democratic institutions against criminal and other extralegal elements.

2. Legitimate Constitutions, Laws and Legal Institutions: Developing constitutions, laws, and institutions derived from democratic processes and consistent with international human rights standards.

3. Strengthened Checks and Balances: Strengthening judicial independence and improving transparency in judicial decision-making and administration, ethics and discipline for all actors in the justice system, and public respect for judicial decision-making.

4. Fairness: Ensuring equal application of the law, procedural fairness, and the protection of basic human rights and civil liberties, and improving both the quantity and quality of justice available to citizens.

5. Effective Application of the Law: Improving the consistent enforcement and application of the law by strengthening administrative systems capacities to carry out core functions and coordination among justice sector actors.

6. Rule of law established in post-conflict environments: Including emergency response to human rights violations, rebuilding core functions within the justice sector, and supporting mechanisms to deal with the legacy of past abuses such as tribunals, truth commissions, and restorative justice mechanisms.

LEADER AWARD:

The leader award consists of two parts: one to support DG "Core" program activities including pilot programs and the other to support possible Department of State and other non-presence country activities. The leader agreement has an authorized funding level of $1.5 million over a five-year life (see expiration date at top).

ASSOCIATE AWARDS:

Missions and Bureaus may negotiate and fund an associate award with no further competition, or separate cooperative agreements or grants to the partner organizations for work in rule of law and human rights. Associate award provisions are thereby loosely analogous to those for task orders under an IQC. There is no limit on the value of individual associate awards, nor a ceiling on the total value of associate awards that may be awarded over the effective life of the leader agreement. Associate awards may extend beyond the life of the lead award.

Missions and Bureaus interested in accessing the services of leader with associate award agreement should contact the AOTR for further details and guidance.

USAID POCs:

CONTACT INFORMATION		
Freedom House (lead organization/ consortium point of contact) Lisa Davis 1301 Connecticut Ave., NW, 6th Floor Washington, DC 20036 Tel: (202) 747-7018 Fax: (202) 296-2840 E-mail: davis@freedomhouse.org Web: www.freedomhouse.org	American Bar Association/Rule of Law Initiative (ABA/ROLI) Michael Maya 740 15th Street, NW Washington, DC 20005 Tel: (202) 662-1974 Fax: (202) 662-1597 E-mail: mmaya@staff.abanet.org Web: www.abanet.org/rol/	National Democratic Institute (NDI) Scott Hubli 2030 M Street, NW, Fifth Floor Washington, DC 20036 Tel: 202-728-6336 Fax: (202) 728-5520 E-mail: shubli@ndi.org Web: www.ndi.org

HUMAN RIGHTS

Respect for human rights
(Program Area 2.1)

Protecting human rights is closely linked to advancing long-term, sustainable development. Rights are both part of the goal of development and instrumental to attaining other goals such as economic growth or democracy. With the creation of the new DRG Center, "human rights" were elevated as a co-equal pillar alongside democracy and governance. USAID's human-rights programming is based on protection, promotion and principles of rights.

Priority Areas: Monitoring human-rights violations; supporting human-rights defenders or commissions; preventing mass atrocities; advancing transitional justice; counter-trafficking in persons (C-TIP); and protecting and promoting the rights of vulnerable populations such as the LGBT community.

Grants Programs :

Human Rights Grant Program
Vulnerable Populations Funds (DCOF/LWVF/VOT/Disabilities/Wheelchairs)

HUMAN RIGHTS GRANT PROGRAM

DRG Contact: Nicole Widdersheim, HGRP Manager

PURPOSE:

With the creation of the new DRG Center, "human rights" were elevated as a co-equal pillar alongside democracy and governance. In order to promote a field focus on human rights, the DRG Center launched a new Human Rights Grants Program (HRGP) in 2012 (then called the Human Rights Fund). The HRGP supports innovative projects that respond to urgent or unanticipated human rights needs or emerging opportunities.

POSSIBLE WORK AREAS:

- The HRGP also strongly encourages agreements with local and regional human rights organizations. The HRGP will also support media and rule-of-law activities insofar as they address human rights problems.

- The HRGP will enable Missions to integrate human rights objectives into current programs and those under design, regardless of sector.

- DRG is seeking, in particular, to collaborate with Missions on specific learning opportunities—for examples impact evaluations and surveys--and to develop best practices in human rights programming.

CONTACT INFORMATION:

Nicole Widdersheim
Program Manager
Tel: (202) 712-5725
Fax: (202) 204-3042
E-mail: nwiddersheim@usaid.gov
Web: https://sites.google.com/a/usaid.gov/drg/funds-mechanisms/hrgp

VULNERABLE POPULATIONS FUNDS

The Vulnerable Populations portfolio works to reduce risks to vulnerable populations, and to reinforce the capacities of communities, local nongovernmental organizations (NGO), and governments to provide services and protection for vulnerable groups. Programs help vulnerable populations gain access to opportunities that support their full participation in society.

Vulnerable Populations comprises five congressionally-directed programs. The Vulnerable Populations team includes personnel with technical expertise in those programming areas, as well as the USAID's Disability Coordinator, who works to ensure that Agency fully complies with its own disability policy. The five programs are:

- Displaced Children and Orphans Fund (DCOF),
- Disability Program,
- Victims of Torture Program (VOT),
- Leahy War Victims Fund (LWVF), and
- Wheelchair Program.

Vulnerable Populations has been at the forefront of developing innovative and state-of-the-art programming for children affected by war, in setting orthopedic and rehabilitation standards in developing countries, and in improving treatment and healing options for survivors of torture. It has also lead worldwide policy change on barrier-free accessibility and inclusion of people with disabilities in family and community.

Each fund has its own purpose and strategy, but they share a focus on providing services to poor and vulnerable people and an emphasis on community. Collectively, Vulnerable Populations conducts programs in more than seventy (70) countries around the world.

DISABILITY PROGRAM

DRG Contact: Rob Horvath (COR)

Technical Support Contract	Award Number	Expiration	Period of Performance
Technical Support Contract	AID-OAA-M-10-00010	09/27/2015	N/A

PURPOSE:

USAID is committed integrating people with disabilities into its programs and activities and to building the capacity of disability organizations that advocate for and offer services on behalf of people with disabilities. This commitment is reinforced by the USAID disability policy and extends from the design and implementation of USAID programming to advocacy for and outreach to people with disabilities.

USAID's policy on disability is to avoid discrimination against people with disabilities in programs which USAID funds and to stimulate an engagement of host-country counterparts, governments, implementing organizations and other donors in promoting a climate of nondiscrimination against and equal opportunity for people with disabilities. The USAID policy ensures that people with disabilities are included at every level, as administrators, partners, and beneficiaries.

POSSIBLE WORK AREAS:

USAID's disability funds are used to support programs and activities to address the needs of people with disabilities, including protecting the rights and increasing the independence and full participation of people with disabilities in programs related to health, education, economic growth, political participation, and humanitarian aid. The Funds' focus is on reducing barriers for people with disabilities in existing USAID programs. The Fund also supports the development and implementation of training for USAID staff and its partners overseas to promote the full inclusion and equal participation of people with disabilities in countries where USAID is present.

This Fund is coordinated and supported by the Office of Democracy and Governance, although most activities are implemented through Mission-managed grants and agreements. The Disability Fund is active in over 30 countries worldwide. As part of its oversight and managerial responsibilities for the Fund, DRG maintains a technical assistance contract with Manila Consulting, Inc. This contract provides technical assistance and support for field Missions that are interested in developing programs under the Fund.

CONTACT INFORMATION:

Catherine Savino, Project Director
Technical Support Contract
Tel: (202) 789-1500
Fax: (202) 204-3042
csavino@usaid.gov

Rob Horvath, Fund Manager
Tel: (202) 712-5239
Fax: (202) 204-3042
E-mail: rhorvath@usaid.gov
Web: www.usaid.gov/about_usaid/disability/

DISPLACED CHILDREN AND ORPHANS FUND

DRG Contact: Rob Horvath (COR)

Technical Support Contract	Award Number	Expiration	Period of Performance
Technical Support Contract	AID-OAA-M-10-00010	09/27/2015	N/A

PURPOSE:
Established in 1988, the Displaced Children and Orphans Fund (DCOF) provides care, support, and protection for the special needs of children at risk, including orphans, unaccompanied minors, children affected by armed conflict, and children with disabilities. Programs center on strengthening the capacity of families and communities to address the physical, social, educational, economic, and emotional needs of children in crisis. The program aims to preserve the family structure; promote the growth and development of vulnerable children; and develop community structures to care, support, and protect vulnerable populations.

POSSIBLE WORK AREAS:
Most DCOF activities are implemented through USAID Mission-managed grants and agreements. A major portion of these Congressionally-mandated funds are used to support programs and activities that provide direct assistance to vulnerable children. DCOF funds also support the design, implementation, and monitoring of programs that provide evidence-based guidance and replicable models for future expansion or replication. DCOF is currently active in 23 countries, including Afghanistan, Armenia, Azerbaijan, Bangladesh, , Burundi, Cambodia, Colombia, Democratic Republic of the Congo, Egypt, Georgia, Guatemala, Indonesia, Kenya, Liberia, Moldova, Mozambique, Nepal, Philippines, Sri Lanka, Tanzania, Thailand, Uganda, and Zambia.

As part of its oversight and managerial responsibilities for the Fund, DRG maintains the SPANS technical assistance contract with Manila Consulting, Inc. This contract provides technical assistance and support for Field Missions that are interested in developing programs under the Fund.

CONTACT INFORMATION:
Catherine Savino, Project Director
SPANS Technical Support Contract
Tel: (202) 789-1500
Fax: (202) 204-3042
E-mail: csavino@usaid.gov

Rob Horvath, Program Manager
Telephone: (202) 712-5239
Fax: (202) 204-3042
E-mail: rhorvath@usaid.gov
Web: www.usaid.gov/our_work/humanitarian_assistance/the_funds/dcof/

VICTIMS OF TORTURE PROGRAM

DRG Contact: Rob Horvath (COR)

Technical Support Contract	Award Number	Expiration	Period of Performance
Technical Support Contract	AID-OAA-M-10-00010	09/27/2015	N/A

PURPOSE:

The Victims of Torture Fund primarily supports programs that help heal the psychological and physical trauma caused by torture, recognizing that communities, along with survivors, need to heal and recover.

The Fund works through non-governmental organizations overseas that: (1) provide direct services to survivors, their families, and communities; (2) strengthen the capacity of country-based institutions in their delivery of services to survivors; and (3) increase the level of knowledge and understanding about the needs of torture victims. These programs include advocacy, training, technical assistance, and research. The Fund is coordinated and supported by the Office of Democracy and Governance, although most activities are Mission-managed grants and agreements. The program currently supports activities in 15 countries including Bangladesh, Cambodia, Cameroon, Democratic Republic of the Congo, Guatemala, Iraq, Kenya, Kosovo, Namibia, Nepal, Pakistan, Rwanda, Sierra Leone, Sri Lanka, and Uganda.

As part of its oversight and managerial responsibilities for the Fund, DRG maintains a technical assistance contract with Manila Consulting, Inc. This contract provides technical assistance and support for Field Missions that are interested in developing programs under the Fund.

CONTACT INFORMATION:

Catherine Savino, Project Director
SPANS Technical Support Contract
Tel: (202) 789-1500
Fax: (202) 204-3042
E-mail: csavino@usaid.gov

Rob Horvath, Program Manager
Telephone: (202) 712-5239
Fax: (202) 204-3042
E-mail: rhorvath@usaid.gov
Web: www.usaid.gov/our_work/humanitarian_assistance/the_funds/vot/

LEAHY WAR VICTIMS FUND (LWVF)

DRG Contact: Rob Horvath (COR)

Technical Support Contract	Award Number	Expiration	Period of Performance
Technical Support Contract	AID-OAA-M-10-00010	09/27/2015	N/A

PURPOSE:

The Leahy War Victims Fund (LWVF) focuses on the needs of civilian victims of conflict in developing countries with the primary objective of expanding access to affordable and appropriate prosthetic/orthotic services. Established in 1989, the program has slowly expanded beyond the provision of essential orthopedic services and related medical, surgical, and rehabilitation assistance to include programs that work to enable amputees and other people with disabilities to regain accessibility to mainstream educational, recreational, and economic opportunities.

POSSIBLE WORK AREAS:

The LWVF is concerned with the provision of orthopedic services and devices to ensure unassisted mobility for civilian war victims and other persons with disabilities in post-conflict countries. Assistance may include training and institutional capacity-strengthening, facilities upgrading, materials provision, and support for national disabilities policy reform and public advocacy. In addition, programs include support for increasing the social and economic opportunities of these survivors.

This fund is coordinated and supported by DRG, although most activities are implemented through Mission-managed grants and agreements. The LWVF is active in Afghanistan, Angola, Cambodia, Colombia, Central America, Democratic Republic of the Congo, Ethiopia, Kenya, Laos, Lebanon, Nepal, Philippines, Sri Lanka, Sudan, Uganda, and Vietnam. As part of its oversight and managerial responsibilities for the Fund, DRG maintains a technical assistance contract with Manila Consulting. This contract provides technical assistance and support for Field Missions that are interested in developing programs under the Fund.

CONTACT INFORMATION:

Catherine Savino, Project Director
Technical Support Contract
Tel: (202) 789-1500
Fax: (202) 204-3042
E-mail: csavino@usaid.gov

Rob Horvath, Program Manager
Telephone: (202) 712-5239
Fax: (202) 204-3042
E-mail: rhorvath@usaid.gov
Web: www.usaid.gov/our_work/humanitarian_assistance/the_funds/lwvf/

WHEELCHAIR PROGRAM

DRG Contact: Rob Horvath (COR)

Technical Support Contract	Award Number	Expiration	Period of Performance
Technical Support Contract	AID-OAA-M-10-00010	09/27/2015	N/A

PURPOSE:

The goal of the Wheelchair Fund is to improve the mobility of people with mobility-related disabilities, which can lead to advances in their overall health. Grantees currently work in many facets of wheelchair provision: researching better, more durable chairs; ensuring appropriate cushions and seating; training to prescribe and fit wheelchairs; and testing and developing international standards.

POSSIBLE WORK AREAS:

Funds are used to support programs that improve access to, availability of, and sustainability of, appropriate wheelchair programs in the developing world. At a broad level, programs contribute to the full and equal participation of people with disabilities in social and economic life. At an implementation level programs aim for, but are not limited to: introducing wheelchairs that are suitable and appropriate for use in developing countries and that are adaptable and fitted to the needs and requirements of each individual; develop and/or increase the capacity of national programs to produce and repair wheelchairs; strengthen human resource capacity to prescribe, fit, and train users; and develop and/or introduce new technologies that are appropriate for local conditions.

This fund is coordinated and supported by DRG, although most activities are implemented through Mission-managed grants and agreements. The program supports activities in eleven countries: Albania, Georgia, Indonesia, Iraq, Kenya, Liberia, Morocco, Nepal, Philippines, Romania, Sierra Leone, and Togo.

As part of its oversight and managerial responsibilities for the Fund, DRG maintains a technical assistance contract with Manila Consulting. This contract provides technical assistance and support for Field Missions that are interested in developing programs under the Fund.

CONTACT INFORMATION:

Catherine Savino, Project Director
Technical Support Contract
Tel: (202) 789-1500
Fax: (202) 204-3042
E-mail: csavino@usaid.gov

Rob Horvath, Program Manager
Telephone: (202) 712-5239
Fax: (202) 204-3042
E-mail: rhorvath@usaid.gov
Web: www.usaid.gov/our_work/humanitarian_assistance/the_funds/lwvf/wheelchairs.html

DRG-RELATED SERVICES HELD IN OTHER USAID BUREAUS OR MISSIONS:*

AmericasBarometer (LAC/RSD)
Capable Partners Program (CAP) (ODP)

*This is not an exhaustive list of DRG-related mechanisms held in other bureaus or Missions.

LAC REGIONAL MECHANISM: AMERICASBAROMETER

Program Areas 2.1-2.4   **LAC Contact:** Vanessa Reilly/Eric Kite

Cooperative Agreements	Award Number	Expiration	Performance Period
Vanderbilt University	598-A-00-06-00061	3/28/2015	N/A

PURPOSE:

Vanderbilt University conducts AmericasBarometer democracy, governance and citizen security surveys in Latin America and Caribbean countries and related country and regional analyses. Country reports and, when requested, "oversampling" reports can be prepared that compare results from areas with USAID-programs to the rest of the country. The biennial survey includes 40,000 survey across 25 countries in the hemisphere. Vanderbilt is also conducting an impact evaluation of the Agency's crime prevention activities under the Central America Regional Security Initiative (CARSI) in Guatemala, El Salvador and Panama.

POSSIBLE WORK AREAS:

The AmericasBarometer series of surveys are of great interest to host country stakeholders, including civil society, media, government officials and citizens; to USAID and the U.S. Government; and to a broader audience that includes political and social scientists and Latin Americanists. The surveys gather data and analyze citizens' perceptions of and experiences with a broad range of important democracy issues, including social capital, political tolerance, local government efficacy, corruption, citizen insecurity and crime, courts, the legislature and the executive. They also include a wide range of behavior variables, including citizen participation and electoral behavior, among others. The effort, which began in a limited way in the 1970s, is directed by Dr. Mitchell Seligson, Vanderbilt University Centennial Professor of Political Science and Fellow of Vanderbilt's Center for the Americas. USAID Missions and other stakeholders can request services such as special survey questions, in-depth country reports, oversamples and dissemination and discussion events.

Public Access to AmericasBarometer Data, Surveys and Reports

All of the AmericasBarometer reports are available to the public on-line in English and Spanish at http://www.vanderbilt.edu/lapop/. The survey data can also be analyzed publicly, at no charge through the same website, with the hopes that students and professionals around the world will conduct additional research and statistical analysis. Several major university libraries serve as data repositories for some or all of the AmericasBarometer data. Published studies have been deposited in libraries throughout the world.

USAID Cooperation with Vanderbilt University

USAID has supported the AmericasBarometer surveys for over 10 years. While the surveys' primary goal is giving the hemisphere's citizens a voice on democracy issues, they also help guide USAID programming, alert policymakers throughout the region to potential problem areas, and inform citizens about democratic values and experiences in their countries relative to regional trends. USAID officers use the AmericasBarometer findings to prioritize funding allocation and guide program design. The surveys are also often employed as an evaluation tool, by comparing results in specialized "oversample" areas with national trends. In March 2006, USAID signed a Cooperative Agreement with Vanderbilt University that supports the project until 2014. The Agreement is managed out of USAID's Bureau for Latin America and the Caribbean (LAC), and contributes about $1 million per year from USAID Missions in the region and the LAC Bureau for survey work, primarily in USAID-presence countries.

CONTACT INFORMATION:

Vanessa Reilly
USAID/LAC
Tel: (202) 712-0133
Email: vreilly@usaid.gov

CAPABLE PARTNERS PROGRAM (CAP) LWA

ODP/OD Contact: Tom Carter (AOR) Zufan Mulugeta (Alternate)

Cooperative Agreement	Award Number	Expiration	Performance Period
FHI 360 consortium	HFP-A-00-03-00020-00	8/10/2013	8/10/2018

PURPOSE:

The Capable Partners Program (CAP) is a USAID Leader with Associates (LWA) Cooperative Agreement managed through the Agency's Office of Development Partners (ODP). CAP is a non-DRG civil society strengthening LWA that works with Missions to strengthen the organizational and technical capacities and sustainability of non-governmental organizations (NGOs), community-based organizations (CBOs), faith-based organizations (FBOs), networks, and intermediate support organizations (ISOs). The current emphasis of the core component of the award is a Local Capacity Enrichment Learning Agenda that seeks to assess a wide variety of approaches to organizational change and offer a series of recommendations for the IDEA/LS Development Grants Program as well as for a broader USAID and donor audience.

POSSIBLE WORK AREAS:

CAP works with Missions to design and implement interventions that are adapted to local contexts and based on proven approaches. CAP's Associate Awards mechanism may be used across the full range of technical sectors. New Associate Awards related to any of CAP's four programmatic objectives may be executed until August 10, 2013. Associate Awards may run until August 10, 2018. Concurrence is more likely for those associate award proposals that emphasize strengthening country and regional support organizations.

- Objective 1: Organizational development (OD), operational and/or technical capacity of local NGOs, networks and ISOs strengthened;
- Objective 2: Linkages among local organizations (NGOs, coops, networks, governments and businesses) strengthened;
- Objective 3: Increased capacity of NGOs, networks and ISOs to engage in advocacy for key policies or programs; and
- Objective 4: Wide dissemination of tested innovations, best practices and lessons learned.

The CAP consortium is led by FHI360 in partnership with Management Systems International (MSI). Other consortium partners are listed below and include several organizations with strong backgrounds in DRG programs:

- The Advocacy Institute
- Aga Khan Foundation, U.S.A.
- The American Red Cross
- Citizens Development Corps
- Freedom from Hunger
- Goodwill Industries International
- The Huairou Commission
- Institute for Multi-Track Diplomacy

- The Kenan Institute
- Mercy Corps
- National Cooperative Business Association
- ORT International Cooperation
- Social Impact

GRANTEE:

Barney Singer, Vice President and Program Director
FHI360
1825 Connecticut Ave., NW
Washington, DC 20009
Tel: (202) 884-8918 /Fax: (202) 884-8442

COORDINATION WITH OTHER USG AGENCIES/PROGRAMS:

FEDERAL JUDICIAL CENTER
FMCS
ICITAP
IJRC
OPDAT

FEDERAL JUDICIAL CENTER

PURPOSE: The Federal Judicial Center's statutory mission includes a mandate to provide information to help improve the administration of justice in foreign countries and to acquire information about the judicial systems of other nations that will improve the administration of justice in the courts of the United States.

*Note: DCHA/DRG has no *official* relationship with the Federal Judicial Center. Information about the Center listed here is intended to serve as a resource for Missions interested in developing or strengthening Rule of Law programming.*

POSSIBLE WORK AREAS:

At the invitation and with the financial support of the U.S. government, foreign judiciaries, or international development organizations, Center staff has visited foreign courts and judicial training centers to participate in conferences and technical assistance projects. This outreach has included judicial and court education programs with the Russian Academy of Justice; a caseload tracking and reporting assessment for the High Court in Lusaka, Zambia; a U.S./Council of Europe judicial reform assessment in Kosovo; and assistance with the implementation of a new case calendaring initiative in Trinidad and Tobago. The International Judicial Relations Office also can identify U.S. Judges, court managers, and public defenders with expertise relevant for a particular international rule of law program or court reform project.

Additionally, each year the Center hosts delegations of judges, attorneys, court officials, and scholars from around the world at its offices in the Thurgood Marshall Federal Judiciary Building in Washington, D.C. These sessions provide information about the United States legal and judicial systems as well as an overview of the Center's education and research activities.

CONTACT INFORMATION:

Federal Judicial Center
Mira Gur-Arie
Director, International Judicial Relations Office
Thurgood Marshall Federal Judiciary Building
One Columbus Circle, NE
Washington, DC 20002-8003
Email: Mgurarie@fjc.gov
Web: www.fjc.gov

FEDERAL MEDIATION & CONCILIATION SERVICE (FMCS)

PURPOSE: The FMCS is an independent federal agency created to promote stable and productive labor-management relationships. In both the U.S. and in developing market economies throughout the world, FMCS delivers innovative approaches to resolving labor-management and workplace conflicts. The Agency's international work is designed to level the global economic playing field for US companies and workers by advocating core labor standards and conflict resolution systems for all nations. Through programs designed to strengthen the rule of law, labor relations and workers' rights, the FMCS helps ensure economic growth and competitiveness.

Note: DCHA/DRG has no official relationship with the Federal Mediation and Conciliation Service. Information about the Agency listed here is intended to serve as a resource for Missions interested in developing or strengthening Rule of Law and/or Civil Society programming.

POSSIBLE WORK AREAS: Through mediator presentations and interactive training, both in the U.S. and abroad, FMCS shares best-practices in the full range of labor-management relations, collective bargaining/negotiations, interest-based problem solving, individual grievance mediation, mediation of collective agreements, and arbitration. FMCS also provides in-depth capacity building through labor relations and dispute resolution systems design, including negotiations, alternative dispute resolution, mediation, arbitration, labor inspector training, and train-the-trainer.

Highly skilled and experienced FMCS mediators can deliver programs such as:

- Dispute Resolution Systems Design – creating and implementing workplace conflict resolution systems;

- Education and Mentoring – training labor, management, and government representatives in industrial relations practices, mediation techniques, negotiation skills, and conflict resolution processes;

- Mediation and Facilitation Services – providing interest-based problem solving techniques and consensus-building dialogue to promote economic growth and legal or institutional reform.

FMCS also provides briefings and other programs for foreign leaders, labor attaches, international delegations, and other foreign visitors on U.S. industrial relations practices and conflict resolution systems. Special tutorials can be arranged for small groups with interest in relationship development and training through observation of FMCS field mediators in actual cases.

CONTACT INFORMATION
Allison Beck
Deputy Director, National and International Programs
Federal Mediation & Conciliation Service
2100 K Street, NW
Washington, DC 20427
Tel: 202-606-8100
Fax: 202-606-4251
Email: abeck@fmcs.gov

INTERNATIONAL CRIMINAL INVESTIGATIVE TRAINING ASSISTANCE PROGRAM (ICITAP)

DRG Contact: Julie Werbel, Tel. 202-712-1711, jwerbel@usaid.gov

PURPOSE:
To promote sustainable institutional development in partnership with host country law enforcement and prosecutorial agencies through technical assistance, mentoring, internships and training. ICITAP is committed to working with USAID to achieve improved governance by taking a holistic approach to addressing crime that includes prevention, intervention and enforcement.

POSSIBLE WORK AREAS:
ICITAP has programs in 40, countries, 20 of which are led by U.S. Government Senior Law Enforcement Advisors. All ICITAP programs are supervised by either federal employees in the field or at headquarters in Washington, D.C. ICITAP can assist USAID by conducting assessments that develop realistic and measurable performance indicators, and by designing and implementing law enforcement development programs. ICITAP has extensive experience in designing and implementing programs in the following topical areas that coincide with USAID priorities and needs: community based policing, respect for human rights and human dignity, community justice, anti-corruption, developing internal affairs capacity within police departments, election security development for police and civil society, forensics development, and anti-trafficking-in-persons programs. Like USAID, ICITAP is committed to promoting the concept of sustainable institutional development.

CONTACT INFORMATION:
International Criminal Investigative Training Assistance Program (ICITAP)
Associate Director Eric Beinhart, on detail to DCHA/DRG or John Buchanan, Deputy Director for Programs
1331 F Street, NW, Suite 500
Washington, DC 20530
Tel: (202) 353-2526
Fax: (202) 616-8429
Email: ebeinhart@usaid.gov or john.buchanan@usaid.govWeb: www.usdoj.gov/criminal/icitap/

INTERNATIONAL JUDICIAL RELATIONS COMMITTEE

DRG Contact: Sara Werth, Tel. 202-712-1946, swerth@usaid.gov

PURPOSE:

Article III Judges comprise the International Judicial Relations Committee (IJRC), which coordinates the federal judiciary's relationship with foreign judiciaries and with official and unofficial agencies and organizations interested in international judicial relations, and the establishment and expansion of the rule of law and the administration of justice.

The Committee also facilitates the development and administration of programs designed to assist foreign judges and court managers such as the translation and dissemination of materials about the United States and its judicial system. The IJRC can also identify U.S. Federal Judges with expertise relevant for a particular international rule of law program or court reform project.

The IJRC is staffed by Senior Attorneys at the Administrative Offices of the US Courts. Together with the USAID Liaison (AOR), the AOUSC provides support to the IJRC for the implementation and coordination of judicial exchanges, judicial reform projects and production of substantive materials for rule of law programs.

POSSIBLE WORK AREAS:

Federal Judges have volunteered their time to support USAID ROL programs in several areas, including but not limited to:

- Establishing or strengthening judicial bodies
- Strengthening judicial administration, management and self-governance
- Enhancing judicial professional development
- Improving transparent and efficient administration of justice system components
- Strengthening the implementation of law and procedures
- Establishing and nurturing long-term relationships with foreign judiciaries undergoing reform

CONTACT INFORMATION:

Administrative Office of the US Courts
Wanda Rubianes
One Columbus Circle, NE
Washington, DC 20544
Tel: (202) 502-1860
Email: wanda_rubianes@ao.uscourts.gov
Web: www.uscourts.gov/adminoff.html

OFFICE OF OVERSEAS PROSECUTORIAL DEVELOPMENT, ASSISTANCE AND TRAINING (OPDAT)

DRG Contact: Julie Werbel, Tel. 202-712-1711, jwerbel@usaid.gov

PURPOSE:

The purpose of the OPDAT is to develop and administer technical assistance designed to enhance the capabilities of foreign justice sector institutions and their law enforcement personnel, so they can effectively partner with the Department of Justice in combating terrorism, trafficking in persons, organized crime, corruption, and financial crimes.

POSSIBLE WORK AREAS:

OPDAT draws on Department of Justice resources and expertise to strengthen foreign criminal justice sector institutions and enhance the administration of justice abroad. OPDAT supports the United States and the Department's law enforcement objectives and priorities by preparing foreign counterparts to cooperate more fully and effectively with the United States in combating terrorism, trafficking in persons, organized crime, corruption, financial crimes, and other transnational crime. It does so by providing technical assistance for legislative and justice sector reform in countries with inadequate laws; by improving the skills of foreign prosecutors and investigators; and by promoting the rule of law and respect for human rights. Active federal prosecutors provide the vast majority of the technical assistance on OPDAT programs.

CONTACT INFORMATION:

Office of Overseas Prosecutorial Development, Assistance and Training (OPDAT)
Carl Alexandre, Director
1331 F Street, NW, Suite 400
Washington, DC 20530
Tel: (202) 616-8388
Fax: (202) 616-8429
Email: carl.alexandre@usdoj.gov
Web: www.usdoj.gov/criminal/opdat/

DRG-RELATED RESOURCES

DRG Relevant Publications, Tools, and Assessments

Democracy, Human Rights and Governance niche organizations in the DC region

DRG RELEVANT PUBLICATIONS, TOOLS, AND ASSESSMENTS

Cross-Cutting

The USAID Democracy and Governance Assessment Framework for Strategy Development

The Democracy and Governance Assessment Framework for Strategy Development provides a framework for constructing US government, in particular USAID, democracy and governance strategies. It is designed to help define a country-appropriate program to assist in the transition to and consolidation of democracy, by addressing the core democracy and governance problem(s) and identifying primary actors and institutions. To achieve this, the framework guides a political analysis of the country and incorporates what researchers and practitioners have learned from comparative experience; it also mandates a realistic look at existing constraints. The final product is a report that provides a set of strategic and programmatic recommendations and their likely impacts on democratic reform. The assessments feed directly into the Country Development Cooperation Strategies, Mission Strategic and Resource Plans, and Operational Plans as well as helping the Mission prioritize its DRG investments for a 3-5 year period.

The assessment process entails sending a few experts in country, who work in close coordination with the Mission for approximately three weeks. For more information, contact Brian Hanley at bhanley@usaid.gov.

Civil Society

Civil Society Assessment Tool

Constituencies for Reform: Strategic Approaches for Donor Supported Civic Advocacy Programs

This document provides guidance to donors in the development of civil society programs in support of promoting democracy and good governance. It outlines a five-step strategic logic for assessing the role of civil society and determining investment priorities for this sector. The first step entails an analysis of major obstacles to democratic political development. Step two is the formulation of a reform agenda to advance good governance. The third step involves a survey of civil society organizations which have interests corresponding with the reform agenda and thereby share a common concern in developing a basis for coalition-building. Step four concentrates on assessing what organizational capacities are needed to strengthen the advocacy role of civil society, and step five identifies what must be done to enhance the capacities and openness of host-country institutions and arenas in which civil society can effectively advance the reform process. For more information, contact Maryanne Yerkes at myerkes@usaid.gov.

Enabling Environment Assessment Tool

NGO Sustainability Index

The NGO Sustainability Index is a key analytical tool that measures the progress of non-governmental organizations (NGOs) in the Europe and Eurasia (E&E) region. The NGO Sustainability Index draws on the expertise of NGO leaders in 29 countries and entities in E&E and highlights major developments and trends in the NGO environment. Seven different dimensions of the NGO sector are analyzed in the NGO Sustainability Index: legal environment, organizational capacity, financial viability, advocacy, service provision, NGO infrastructure and public image. In the Index, each of these dimensions is examined with a focus on the following questions: (1) What has been accomplished? (2) What remains a problem? (3) Do local actors recognize the nature of outstanding challenges? (4) Do the local actors have a strategy and the capacity to address these challenges? Scores are measured on a 1 to 7 scale, with 7 indicating a low or poor level of development and 1 indicating a very advanced level of progress. Each country report provides an in-depth analysis of the NGO sector along with comparative information regarding prior years' dimension scores encapsulated in easy-to-read charts. For more information, contact Maryanne Yerkes at MYerkes@usaid.gov

Enabling Environment Assessment Tool
ICNL tools and guides
The International Center for Not-for-Profit Law (ICNL) offers several tools helpful to assessing the enabling environment for civil society organizations. "Safeguarding Civil Society in Politically Complex Environments" is an informative 26-page desk study produced by ICNL with USAID funding in 2007 (www.icnl.org/knowledge/ijnl/vol9iss3/special_1.htm). The article seeks to identify available strategies and tools to protect civil society and freedom of association in politically complex environments. This working document discusses use of the following strategies, tools, and mechanisms: (a) protective alliances and networks; (b) raising public awareness; (c) advocacy campaigning; (d) direct public action; (e) international diplomacy; (f) domestic litigation; (g) national and international human rights mechanisms; (h) legal triage; and (i) going underground. ICNL also provides a "Checklist for CSO Laws" on its website (www.icnl.org/knowledge/pubs/NPOChecklist.pdf) that outlines provisions that should be included in legislation governing civil society organizations (CSOs). The list is useful for assessing whether CSO legislation currently on the books or in draft form meets generally accepted international practices. For more information, contact Douglas B. Rutzen at ICNL at drutzen@icnl.org or contact Patricia Hunter at PHunter@usaid.gov .

Labor Sector Assessment Tool and Programming Handbook – new website
Global Labor Sector Analytic Initiative (2010)
The Labor Sector and U.S. Foreign Assistance Goals
The new Global Labor Sector Analytic Initiative (GLaSAI) website provides a dynamic knowledge bank about the impact of the labor sector on political, social, and economic development. Recognizing that labor sector issues affect many of the most pressing development needs such as livelihoods, human rights, competitiveness, human trafficking, and HIV/AIDS, among others, the GLaSAI website provides access to the research, tools, experts, and technical assistance needed to design, implement, and evaluate labor sector programming in the context of country-specific or global objectives. Practical findings of the analytic initiative are presented for policy makers, country team leaders, technical officers, implementing partners, and researchers in the short paper "Why Labor Matters." For more information, go to http://www.glasai.com/.

Media Programming Tool
The Role of Media in Democracy: A Strategic Approach
This guide outlines a menu of implementation options for media programming that can be selected for adaptation to country context and available resources. The guide describes potential actors involved in media programming, weaknesses that may require attention, and strategies for strengthening the independent media sector. Illustrative activities include: journalism training; building country capacity for training media professionals; strengthening business capacities of media or capital infusions to media enterprises; media law reform and advocacy; supporting development of media sector CSOs; and more. For more information, contact Mark Koenig at mkoenig@usaid.gov.

Youth Assessment Tool
Youth and Extremism Assessment Module
This tool is intended to facilitate the collection and analysis of data related to the nexus between youth and extremism. The tool may be used within the context of a country-specific cross-sectoral youth assessment or as a stand-alone data collection instrument. It consists of targeted questions meant to focus attention on key variables and issues, and proceeds in five steps: (1) Lays the basis for a general profile of the at-risk youth population

(nature, level, and geographical location of the threat); (2) Seeks to understand the motivations that may prompt youth to join, or become loosely affiliated with, radicalized groups and organizations; (3) Develops an understanding of the conditions that shape the ability of organizations to recruit, organize and operate among the youth and how these steps take place; (4)Assesses the main trends that may be affecting the scope and nature of the extremism threats to youth; and (5) Provides guidelines for strategy development, based on the results of the analysis conducted in steps 1 through 4. For more information, contact Maryanne Yerkes at myerkes@usaid.gov.

Media Programming Under Fragile Conditions: A Democracy and Governance Program Guide (2009)

The media play a vital role in many developing countries. Media outlets enable citizens to communicate with each other, serve as platforms for debate, anchor democratic processes, and facilitate poverty reduction and development through provision of needed information. In states experiencing conflict, violent political upheaval, or complete collapse, the media sector is even more critical.

http://cms1.usaid.gov/DG/TA/CS/upload/media_programming_guide.pdf

A Mobile Voice: The Use of Mobile Phones in Citizen Media (2008)

This publication explores the dynamics of the role of mobile phones in enhancing access to and creating information for citizen-produced media.

www.usaid.gov/our_work/democracy_and_governance/publications/pdfs/Mobile_Voice_Citizen_Media.pdf

Civil Society Groups and Political Parties: Supporting Constructive Relationships (2004)

This paper deals with two broad sets of questions. First, what do we think we should be aiming for at the systemic level, in terms of the relationship between civil society and political parties? Second, in a given setting, what kinds of relationships, at the micro level (among individual organizations), can contribute to democratization?

www.usaid.gov/our_work/democracy_and_governance/publications/pdfs/constituencies.pdf

Mitigating Abusive Labor Conditions: Contemporary Strategies and Lessons Learned (2003)

This paper describes a sample of the existing anti-sweatshop programs, assesses the strengths and weaknesses of each, and provides a set of recommendations for future directions in combating sweatshops.

www.usaid.gov/our_work/democracy_and_governance/publications/pdfs/pnacu630.pdf

Approaches to Civic Education: Lessons Learned (2002)

This document reports on lessons learned from a research investigation into USAID's civic education programming.

www.usaid.gov/our_work/democracy_and_governance/publications/pdfs/pnacp331.pdf

The Enabling Environment for Free & Independent Media: Contribution to Transparent & Accountable Governance (2002)

This document identifies the main components of the legal environment that enable media to advance democratic goals.

www.usaid.gov/our_work/democracy_and_governance/publications/pdfs/pnacm006.pdf

The Role of Media in Democracy: A Strategic Approach (1999)

This strategic approach is intended to help USAID field staff make informed decisions with regard to programming media development activities. It analyzes a history of USAID involvement in this area and outlines lessons learned.

www.usaid.gov/our_work/democracy_and_governance/publications/pdfs/pnace630.pdf

Electoral Security Framework: Technical Guidance Handbook for Democracy and Governance Officers (2010)

http://pdf.usaid.gov/pdf_docs/PNAEA453.pdf

The Electoral Security Framework is a diagnostic instrument that profiles electoral conflict for the development of program strategies and activities to prevent, manage or mediate this conflict. It provides USAID Democracy and Governance Officers with an "Assessment—Planning—Programming—Monitoring & Evaluation" methodology for elections and security work. The Handbook is available for hardcopy and electronic distribution. For more information, please contact Tess McEnery at tmcenery@usaid.gov.

Electoral Security Best Practices Guide (2013)

http://www.usaid.gov/sites/default/files/documents/2496/Electoral_Security_Best_Practices_USAID.pdf

The Electoral Security Best Practices Guide is a companion piece to USAID's Electoral Security Framework which synthesizes information gathered from multiple electoral security assessments conducted since the debut of the Framework in 2010. By providing a global overview of best practices in programming to prevent, manage, and/or mediate electoral conflict and violence, the Guide will enable DRG practitioners and partners to cross-reference the country context in which they are programming, and leverage best practices used in similar environments and phases of the electoral cycle. For more information, please contact Tess McEnery at tmcenery@usaid.gov.

USAID Political Party Assistance Policy (2003)

http://pdf.usaid.gov/pdf_docs/PDABY359.pdf

USAID's Political Party Assistance Policy was created in 2003 and is a mandatory reference to ADS 200. Support for political parties overseas remains a long-term interest of the United States. Assistance in strengthening political parties – both in government and in opposition – is one important way the United Sates can support democratization in transitional societies. The goals of USAID's Political Party Assistance are to: 1) development and consolidate representative democracies; 2) develop transparent political environments; 3) establish viable democratic parties; and 4) ensure conduct of free and fair elections. The two guiding principles governing USAID's assistance policy are: USAID programs support representative multi-party systems and USAID programs do not seek to determine election outcomes. For additional details on policy guidelines, prohibited activities, exceptions and implementation guidance, please contact Catie Lott at clott@usaid.gov.

Managing Assistance in Support of Political & Electoral Processes (2000)

http://pdf.usaid.gov/pdf_docs/PNACF631.pdf

This publication helps democracy and governance field officers anticipate and effectively deal with the myriad of issues and challenges that arise with election assistance programs in changing environments. The practical manual guides users through defining the problem and assessing contextual factors; identifying stakeholders and their motives; selecting options for assistance; linking those options to the mission strategy; and managing electoral assistance. It is suggestive rather than directive, in recognition that, while a certain "conventional wisdom" based on years of experience exists about elections programming, the multitude of variables precludes a "one size fits all" approach. The approaches suggested in this handbook are based on material gathered through a year-long assessment of electoral assistance activities carried out by USAID Missions and their partners over the past eight years.

USAID Political Party Development Assistance (1999)

http://pdf.usaid.gov/pdf_docs/PNACE500.pdf

The document provides a clearer understanding of the substance and breadth of USAID political party development assistance, the statutory and political constraints on such USAID-supported programming, the methods and approaches to political party assistance programming by key implementing partners, and the limitations and possibilities for future political party development assistance around the world.

Transition Elections and Political Processes in Reconstruction and Stabilization Operations: Lessons Learned; A Guide for United States Government Planners (November 2007, Office of the Coordinator for Reconstruction and Stabilization)

http://pdf.usaid.gov/pdf_docs/PCAAB804.pdf

This guide is a primer for USG officials so that decisions on elections and political parties are informed by best practices and lessons from roughly two decades of prior experience. The guide should inform strategic-level planning and on-the-ground implementation decisions. Unlike many other guides, it focuses on the election process as well as political parties and voters in pre-election, election-day, and post-election settings. Many of the standard lessons on elections and political processes do not apply, or apply differently, to elections in R&S environments. This guide attempts to capture those differences. It emphasizes how the ensemble of USG resources can best be brought to bear on the election process in R&S operations – which spans from the negotiations over a peace agreement to after the election event. The guide is organized into four sections. The first section presents policy considerations that commonly arise in transitional elections and political processes. The second section presents the elements of strategic planning. The third section highlights best practices in implementation. A final section highlights monitoring and evaluation.

Money in Politics Handbook: A Guide to Increasing Transparency in Emerging Democracies (2003)

http://pdf.usaid.gov/pdf_docs/PNACR223.pdf

As USAID's first publication on political finance in emerging democracies, its purpose is to increase understanding by USAID field staff, host-country political leaders, civil society organizations, and the media of the sometimes obscure and sensitive topic of political finance. It also creates awareness of the issues and benefits of open finances and suggests some practical technical assistance options that encourage the use of disclosure as a methodology for strengthening national democratic political processes.

Vote Count Verification: A User's Guide for Funders, Implementers, and Stakeholders

http://www.democracyinternational.com/sites/default/files/DI%20VCV%20Study%20(2011).pdf

USAID commissioned a comprehensive review and assessment of vote count verification (VCV) techniques, including statistically based and comprehensive parallel vote tabulations (PVTs or "quick counts"), exit polls, public opinion surveys, and postelection statistical analyses. The User's Guide reviews the experiences with vote count verification in recent transitional or post-conflict elections and makes recommendations on the advantages and disadvantages of various verification techniques, depending on the project's specific objectives and the nature of the relevant political environment.

The Declaration of Principles for International Election Observation

http://www.ndi.org/files/DoP-ENG.pdf

The Declaration of Principles for International Election Observation and the Code of Conduct for International Election Observers were developed through a multi-year process involving more than 20 intergovernmental and international nongovernmental organizations concerned with election observation around the world. The declaration was commemorated at the UN in 2005, and is now endorsed by 42 intergovernmental and international organizations, which are engaged in the process of improving international election observation.

Declaration of Global Principles for Nonpartisan Election Observation and Monitoring by Citizen Organizations

http://www.gndem.org/sites/default/files/declaration/Declaration_of_Global_Principles_0.pdf

The Declaration of Global Principles for Nonpartisan Election Observation and Monitoring by Citizen Organizations and Code of Conduct for Non-Partisan Citizen Election Observers and Monitors was drafted by representatives of civil society organizations from Africa, Asia, Central and Eastern Europe, Eurasia, Latin America and the Caribbean, and the Middle East that belong to the Global Network of Domestic Election Monitors. They establish the first voluntary global standards for domestic election observation.

African Election Toolkit

http://cas.state.gov/afelectionstoolkit/

This on-line toolkit, created by the Department of State's Africa Bureau and the Bureau of Democracy, Human Rights, and Labor and USAID, provides resources, templates and examples for analysis and planning by USAID Mission and Embassies appropriate for each stage of the entire electoral cycle and links to external sources of additional information. Designed for an African context, many of the materials are equally applicable for understanding elections in any location.

Governance

Interagency Security Sector Assessment Framework (ISSAF)

U.S. security is enhanced by democratic security sector governance worldwide. There is a growing awareness among security sector experts that a limited focus on improving law and order is not enough; fundamental reforms may be required. Such reforms may include structural changes in security policies, restructuring security sector organizations to improve their functioning, and ensuring that civilian authorities have the capacity to manage and oversee security organizations. The ISSAF is a tool that enables a USAID or interagency team to assess security and justice concerns in states in every stage of development. It can function as a stand-alone tool, as a complement to other related topical frameworks (e.g., the Rule of Law Strategic Framework), or as a sectoral link to other types of broader assessment tools (e.g., the Interagency Conflict Assessment Framework (ICAF)). The ISSAF is divided into two parts: i) a ten-step framework for analysis; and ii) areas of inquiry with illustrative questions. http://www.usaid.gov/our_work/democracy_and_governance/publications/pdfs/ISSAF_October-29_2010.pdf

Maritime Security Sector Reform (MSSR) Guide

The maritime is vulnerable to a wide array of threats, to include illegal, unreported and unregulated fishing; environmental degradation; smuggling; trafficking in persons; narcotics trafficking; piracy; proliferation of weapons of mass destruction; and aggressive actions, including terrorism. The MSSR Guide is an analytical tool designed to map and assess the maritime sector; to assess existing maritime security sector capabilities and gaps; and/or to enable coordination and collaboration to improve maritime safety and security. It can be used to support a full-scale maritime sector assessment; to obtain a snapshot of one or more aspects of a country's maritime sector; or to facilitate discussion among national actors with maritime responsibilities. The Guide is designed to be used in conjunction with other tools, particularly when more in depth treatment of a function or capability may be warranted. http://www.usaid.gov/our_work/democracy_and_governance/publications/pdfs/Maritime-Security-Sector-Reform.pdf

Democratic Decentralization Programming Handbook (June 2009)

The Democratic Decentralization Programming Handbook (DDPH) is designed to facilitate the design, development, implementation and evaluation of USAID decentralization and local government support projects. It is a "second generation" technical leadership product that encourages USAID missions to design decentralization and local government support projects tailored to USG and host-country goals and to relevant country circumstances.
www.usaid.gov/our_work/democracy_and_governance/publications/pdfs/DDPH_09_22_09_508c.pdf

USAID Program Brief: Reducing Corruption in the Judiciary (June 2009)

The linkages between poverty reduction, economic growth, and democratic governance are firmly established in current development thinking, backed by persuasive research. Equally well established is the recognition by scholars, policy makers, and development practitioners of the central importance of the rule of law and the control of corruption successfully addressing the related challenges of social, economic and political development. This program brief specifically addresses efforts to reduce corruption in the judiciary. In its references to "judicial corruption" it includes corrupt acts by judges, prosecutors, public defenders, court officials, and lawyers who are intimately involved in the operation of the judicial system. It recognizes, however, that addressing judicial corruption requires attention to the broader context of corruption in the entire justice system, including law enforcement agencies, and in the society as a whole.

www.usaid.gov/our_work/democracy_and_governance/publications/pdfs/Reducing_Corruption_Judiciary_June09.pdf

Joint Statement on Security Sector Reform (2009)

In early January, USAID, the Department of State, and the Department of Defense issued a joint statement on Security Sector Reform (SSR). This paper responds to a gap in current foreign assistance approaches to security and development. U.S. security assistance programs have sometimes focused too exclusively on providing equipment and training to security forces. However, forces enhanced through traditional assistance can better carry out their responsibilities if the institutional and governance frameworks necessary to sustain them are equally well-developed and equipped. Similarly, development assistance has generally excluded security-related assistance. Yet, development cannot thrive without basic security. The increasingly complex threats facing our partners and our own nation urgently require that we address the linkages among security, governance, development, and conflict in more comprehensive and sustainable ways.

In addition to building professional security forces, SSR supports the establishment of relevant legal and policy frameworks; enhanced civilian management, leadership, oversight, planning and budgeting capacities; and improved coordination and cooperation among security-related and civil institutions.

The paper identifies key principles and recommendations for joint activity. It will be followed by Agency-specific implementation guidelines. For more information, contact Julie Werbel at jwerbel@usaid.gov or see the paper online at http://www.usaid.gov/our_work/democracy_and_governance/publications/pdfs/SSR_JS_Mar2009.pdf

USAID Anticorruption Assessment Handbook (2009)

The Anticorruption Assessment Handbook provides assessment teams with tools for diagnosing the underlying causes of corruption by analyzing both the state of laws and institutions, as well as the political-economic dynamics of a country. The main objective of the assessment approach outlined in this handbook is to assure that assessments start by casting a wide analytical net to capture the breadth of issues that affect corruption and anticorruption prospects in a country and then provide a clearly-justified, strategic rationale for their final programmatic recommendations. This handbook provides step-by-step practical assistance to implement the methodology and produce an assessment report that addresses a wide range of issues and generates recommendations for action. For more information, visit

http://www.usaid.gov/our_work/democracy_and_governance/technical_areas/anticorruption_handbook/index.html or contact Christina del Castillo at cdelcastillo@usaid.gov.

Website on Implementing Policy Change

This website contains a series of documents written as part of USAID's Implementing Policy Change (IPC) program, which provided technical assistance in developing countries around the world to improve policy implementation and democratic governance.   These documents include case studies, short technical notes that describe management tools and approaches, working papers, articles and research on efforts to strengthen the ability and capacity of democratically elected governments to pursue critical political, economic, social, and administrative changes and reforms in their country. These documents contain a wealth of knowledge regarding how to manage change in development contexts.

www.usaid.gov/our_work/democracy_and_governance/publications/ipcindex.html

USAID Program Brief: Anticorruption and Policy Integrity (May 2007)

As part of USAID's technical leadership on security sector reform issues, this program brief discusses the issues surrounding police corruption and offers programmatic guidelines and tools for addressing police corruption. The program brief is designed to "unpack" police corruption contextually, and to identify specific concerns that - in light of the societal role and special powers of the police - should be considered when developing programmatic responses.

http://www.usaid.gov/our_work/democracy_and_governance/publications/pdfs/AC_and_Police_Integrity.pdf

Anticorruption Program Brief: Anticorruption Agencies (2006)

This program brief on Anticorruption Agencies (ACAs) is intended to assist the field by outlining the critical questions around the establishment and workings of a host country's ACA. Since the 1990s, more than 30 countries have established some form of anticorruption agency or commission as a key tactic in their efforts to fight corruption. USAID Missions and other international donors are faced with many questions as they provide advice and assistance to host country governments on their efforts to combat corruption. The document also provides substantive input on how the answers to those questions may affect the effectiveness of donor support for an ACA.

www.usaid.gov/our_work/democracy_and_governance/publications/pdfs/ACA_508c.pdf

USAID Anticorruption Strategy (January 2005)

This document outlines USAID's strategy and approaches to addressing corruption and increasing transparency in the public sector. The Agency's work reduces opportunities and incentives for corruption; supports stronger and more independent judiciaries, legislatures, and oversight bodies; and promotes independent media, civil society, and public education. Corruption, defined as the abuse of entrusted authority for private gain, remains a tremendous obstacle to political, social, and economic development, and efforts to reduce it need to be more fully integrated across all sectors. Decreasing corruption is an important U.S. foreign policy objective. USAID's programs can help target the critical problem of corruption in all its manifestations.

www.usaid.gov/our_work/democracy_and_governance/publications/pdfs/ac_strategy_final.pdf

USAID Handbook on Legislative Strengthening (February 2000)

This handbook is designed to assist USAID Missions in developing strategies to help legislatures function more effectively and to perform their functions more democratically. It explains the importance of legislatures in a democracy, describes factors that influence legislative behavior, and enumerates problems legislatures commonly face. It then presents an assessment framework that is designed to help USAID field officers pinpoint the weaknesses and understand the capabilities of their host-country legislatures. The paper identifies a number of assistance activities designed to address weaknesses and to capitalize on strengths discovered in the assessment. It concludes with guidance for implementing legislative programs and a presentation of emerging issues.

www.usaid.gov/our_work/democracy_and_governance/publications/pdfs/pnacf632.pdf

Rule of Law

A Field Guide for USAID DRG Officers: Assistance to Civilian Law Enforcement in Developing Countries (January 2011)

This field guide, designed for DRG officers considering police assistance programs in their countries, establishes the importance of public safety as a cornerstone of successful development.

http://www.usaid.gov/our_work/democracy_and_governance/publications/pdfs/AFieldGuideforUSAIDDemocracyGovernance%20Officers.pdf

Guide to Rule of Law Country Analysis: The Rule of Law Strategic Framework (Revised 2010)

This guide provides a conceptual framework for analyzing challenges to the rule of law, as well as guidelines for conducting a justice sector assessment and for designing and prioritizing program interventions.
http://www.usaid.gov/our_work/democracy_and_governance/publications/pdfs/ROL_Strategic_Framework_Jan-2010_FINAL.pdf.

Using Administrative Law Tools and Concepts to Strengthen USAID Programming (2008)

This guide introduces administrative law mechanisms and concepts and shows how administrative law can strengthen USAID's DRG programming.
pdf.usaid.gov/pdf_docs/PNADK999.pdf

USAID Policy Guidance for Assistance for Civilian Policing (2005)

This guidance elaborates key points and legislative guidance, notification guidance, program guidelines and advice on implementation, and illustrative activities.
pdf.usaid.gov/pdf_docs/PDACG022.pdf.

Guide for Promoting Judicial Independence and Impartiality (2002)

This guide promotes an understanding of judicial independence and assists USAID in the design and implementation of programs that strengthen it.
pdf.usaid.gov/pdf_docs/PNACM007.pdf

Case Tracking and Management Guide (2001)

This manual provides practical guidance on successful court case tracking and management (CTM) improvement projects.
pdf.usaid.gov/pdf_docs/PNACM001.pdf

Alternative Dispute Resolution Practitioner's Guide (1998)

This guide is intended to help practitioners make informed decisions with regard to incorporating alternative dispute resolution (ADR) in rule of law programs and other conflict management initiatives. It is available on line at
pdf.usaid.gov/pdf_docs/PNACB895.pdf

Special Programs to Address the Needs of Survivors (SPANS)

All SPANS-related publications and tools can be found on the SPANS website. The website includes descriptions of four of SPANS' five Congressional directives: 1) Displaced Children and Orphans Fund; 2) War Victims Fund; 3) Victims of Torture Program; and 4) Wheelchair Program. Users can also find a collection of more than 75 country and special-interest reports produced by SPANS programs since their inception. These publications include in-depth analyses of country programs and descriptions of best practices and lessons learned. See
www.usaid.gov/our_work/humanitarian_assistance/the_funds/index.html for more information.

Information on SPANS' fifth Congressional directive, the Disability program, can be found at
http://www.usaid.gov/about_usaid/disability/index.html. The website offers links to the following Agency policies regarding people with disabilities:
1. Background on USAID and Inclusive Development
2. Promoting Disability Inclusion in USAID Missions

3. Checklist for Inclusion
4. Disability Assessment Tool/Guide
5. Disability Inclusion Plan Table
6. AAPD 04-17 Supporting USAID's Disability Policy in Contracts, Grants, and Cooperative Agreements
7. AAPD 05-07 Supporting USAID's Standards for Accessibility for the Disabled in Contracts, Grants, and Cooperative Agreements
8. USAID Disability Policy Paper
9. Final report of the Ad Hoc Committee on a Comprehensive and Integral International Convention on the Protection and Promotion of the Rights and Dignity of Persons with Disabilities (192.28kb)

Highlights of SPANS reports include:

Fifth Report on the Implementation of USAID Disability Policy. This report describes USAID Missions' redoubled efforts to integrate people with disabilities into their programs and to develop more specific programs that promote equality for and empowerment of people with disabilities. The report further shows that the Agency remains committed to serving as an international leader in the area of inclusive development and to working proactively to remove barriers that may limit the full participation of people with disabilities in family, community, and society. The full report can be accessed at: http://pdf.usaid.gov/pdf_docs/PDACM100.pdf.

Guidelines on the Provision of Manual Wheelchairs in Less- Resourced Settings, found at:
http://whqlibdoc.who.int/publications/2008/9789241547482_eng.pdf

Report of a Consensus Conference on Wheelchairs for Developing Countries, found at:
http://www.who.int/disabilities/technology/Wheelchair_full_report.pdf

Learning Team

Deepening Our Understanding of the Effects of US Foreign Assistance on Democracy Building-Final Report (2008)

A prestigious U.S. academic team examined democratic patterns in 165 countries throughout the world from 1990 to 2004, finding that USAID democracy, human rights and governance (DRG) assistance had a significant positive impact on democratic development. Specifically, the studies conclude that, in any given year, $10 million of USAID DRG funding produces about a five-fold increase in the amount of democratic change over what the average country would otherwise be expected to achieve.

Link to four page summary:
www.usaid.gov/our_work/democracy_and_governance/publications/pdfs/SORA_pitt_vandy4pager_FINAL.pdf
Link to full study:
www.usaid.gov/our_work/democracy_and_governance/publications/pdfs/SORA_FinalReport_June08_508c.pdf
Link to more information, including the database and an earlier study:
www.pitt.edu/~politics/democracy/democracy.html.

Improving Democracy Assistance: Building Knowledge Through Evaluations and Research (2008)

Through a contract awarded in 2006 to the National Academy of Sciences (NAS), an expert commission was convened and a report was produced with recommendations for improving USAID evaluations of DRG programs. The report includes a range of specific practical and policy recommendations that can be implemented by USAID.

Link to four page summary:
www.usaid.gov/our_work/democracy_and_governance/publications/pdfs/SORA_Improving_Democracy_Assistance_Brief.pdf

Link to purchase full report: www.nap.edu/catalog.php?record_id=12164.

DEMOCRACY, HUMAN RIGHTS AND GOVERNANCE NICHE ORGANIZATIONS IN THE DC REGION

USAID/KSC Contact: Michael Ardovino, Ph.D.

Below is a list of mostly non-profit (501) organizations and think-tanks in the Washington DC area that focus on issues related to the democracy, human rights and governance sector and subsectors of rule of law, governance, civil society, and elections, including human rights and natural resources management.

The Advocacy Project
http://www.advocacynet.org/

Advocates for Youth
http://www.advocatesforyouth.org/

Alliance for Peacebuilding
http://www.allianceforpeacebuilding.org/

American Bar Association- Rule of Law Initiative
http://www.abanet.org/rol/about.shtml

Amnesty International
http://www.amnesty.org/

Ashburn Institute
http://www.iaud.org/

Asia Foundation
http://asiafoundation.org/

Association for the Study of the Cuban Economy
http://lanic.utexas.edu/project/asce/

Atlantic Council
http://www.acus.org/about

Brookings
http://www.brookings.edu/about.aspx

Business and Professional Women's Foundation
http://www.bpwusa.org/i4a/pages/index.cfm?pageid=1

Campaign Finance Institute
http://www.cfinst.org/

Carnegie Endowment for International Peace
http://www.carnegieendowment.org/about/

Center for American Progress
http://www.americanprogress.org/

Center for Community Corrections
http://centerforcommunitycorrections.org/

Center for Individual Rights
http://www.cir-usa.org/index.html

Center for International Policy
http://www.ciponline.org/

Center for Progressive Leadership
http://www.progressiveleaders.org/

Center for Public Accountability
http://www.politicalaccountability.net/

Center for Development and Population Activities (CEDPA)
http://www.cedpa.org/

Center for Media and Public Affairs (CMPA)
http://www.cmpa.com/about.htm

Center for the Economic Analysis of Law (CEAL)
http://www.ceal.org/welcome.asp

Center for Global Development (CGD)
http://www.cgdev.org/section/about/

Center for Strategic and International Studies (CSIS)
http://csis.org/about-us

Change to Win
http://www.changetowin.org/

CHF International
http://www.chfinternational.org/node/28011

Citizen Advocacy Center
http://www.cacenter.org/cac/about_cac

CIVICUS (World Alliance for Citizen Participation)
http://www.civicus.org/civicus-home

Coalition of Black Trade Unionists
http://www.cbtu.org/

Committee for Citizen Awareness
http://www.citizenawareness.org/main.html

Consortium for Citizens with Disabilities
http://www.c-c-d.org/

Council on Foreign Relations (CFR)
http://www.cfr.org/about/mission.html

Council of State Governments
http://www.csg.org/

Creative Associates International
http://www.creativeassociatesinternational.com

Criminal Justice Policy Foundation
http://cjpf.org/

Cultural Survival
http://www.culturalsurvival.org/home

Democracy Coalition Project
http://www.demcoalition.org/site09-2008/2005_html/home.html

Democracy International
http://www.democracyinternational.com/

Due Process of Law Foundation
http://www.dplf.org/index.php?IID=12

Earth Council Geneva
http://earthcouncil.com/ecgsite/content/view/3/6/

Ecological Society of America
http://www.esa.org/aboutesa/

The Enough Project
http://www.enoughproject.org/

Environmental Law Institute
http://www.eli.org/

Environmental Integrity Project
http://www.environmentalintegrity.org/

Equal Justice Works
http://www.equaljusticeworks.org/about/mission

Fair Labor Association
http://www.fairlabor.org/

Food and Water Watch
http://www.foodandwaterwatch.org/

Foundation for Criminal Justice (NACDL)
http://www.nacdl.org/public.nsf/freeform/foundation?OpenDocument

Foundation for Defense of Democracies
http://www.defenddemocracy.org/

Freedom House
http://freedomhouse.org/

Friends of the Earth
http://www.foe.org/

Geneva Centre for the Democratic Control of Armed Forces (DCAF)
http://www.dcaf.ch/

Genocide Intervention Network
http://www.genocideintervention.net/

Global Integrity
http://www.globalintegrity.org/aboutus/index.cfm

Global Rights
http://www.globalrights.org/site/PageServer?pagename=index

Human Rights Campaign
http://www.hrc.org/

Human Rights Watch
http://www.hrw.org/

Idealist.org (Action without Borders)
http://www.idealist.org/en/about/mission.html

Institute for Women's Policy Research
http://www.iwpr.org/index.cfm

InterAction
http://www.interaction.org/

Inter-American Dialogue
http://www.thedialogue.org/

International Budget Partnership (IBP)
http://www.internationalbudget.org/

International Center for Not-For-Profit Law (ICNL)
http://www.icnl.org/

International Foundation for Electoral Systems
http://www.ifes.org/

International Institute for Democracy and Electoral Assistance (International IDEA)
http://www.idea.int/about/index.cfm

International Centre for the Prevention of Crime
http://www.crime-prevention-intl.org/

International Center for Research on Women
http://www.icrw.org/

International City/County Managers Association
http://icma.org/en/icma/home

The International Republican Institute
http://www.iri.org/

International Women's Media Foundation
http://www.iwmf.org/

Internews
http://www.internews.org/about/default.shtm

Kudirat Initiative for Democracy
http://www.kind.org/archive/home.html

League of Conservation Voters (LCV)
http://www.lcv.org/about-lcv/

League of Women Voters
http://www.lwv.org//AM/Template.cfm?Section=Home

MADRE
http://www.madre.org/index.php?s=1&b=1

Migration Policy Institute (MPI)
http://www.migrationpolicy.org/about/index.php

National Association for Legal Career Professionals
http://www.nalp.org/mission

National Association of Attorneys General Mission Foundation (NAAG)
http://www.naag.org/about_naag.php

National Association of Broadcasters
http://www.nab.org/AM/Template.cfm?Section=About_NAB

National Association of Broadcasters Education Foundation (NABEF)
http://www.nab.org/AM/Template.cfm?Section=Who_We_Are

National Association of Clean Water Agencies
http://www.nacwa.org/index.php?option=com_content&view=article&id=2&Itemid=9

National Association of Counties
http://www.naco.org/Pages/default.aspx

National Association of Criminal Defense Attorneys
http://www.criminaljustice.org/public.nsf/freeform/publicwelcome?opendocument

National Association of Women Judges
http://www.nawj.org/

National Conference of State Legislatures
http://www.ncsl.org/

National Coalition on Black Civic Participation (NCBCP)
http://www.ncbcp.org/

National Democratic Institute (NDI)
http://ndi.org/

National Juvenile Defense Center
http://www.njdc.info/about_us.php

National Governors Association
http://www.nga.org/portal/site/nga/menuitem.b14a675ba7f89cf9e8ebb856a11010a0

National League of Cities
http://www.nlc.org/inside_nlc/aboutnlc.aspx

National Legal Aid and Defender Association
http://www.nlada.org/About/About_Home

National Women's Law Center
http://www.nwlc.org/

Nature Conservancy
http://www.nature.org/aboutus/?src=t5

Ocean Conservancy
http://www.oceanconservancy.org/site/PageServer?pagename=abt_aboutus

Oceana
http://www.oceana.org/north-america/home/

OneWorld Online
http://us.oneworld.net/

Partners for Democratic Change
http://www.partnersglobal.org/

Plan USA
http://www.planusa.org/planhistory

Police Foundation
http://www.policefoundation.org/

Public Forum Institute
http://www.publicforuminstitute.org/

Quality Education for Minorities
http://www.qem.org/

Radio Free Asia
http://www.rfa.org/english/

Reporters Without Borders (Reporters Sans Frontieres)
http://www.rsf.org/rubrique.php3?id_rubrique=20

Researchers for the Future
http://www.rff.org/Pages/default.aspx

Results for Development Institute
http://resultsfordevelopment.org/index.php

Rights Action
http://www.rightsaction.org/

Rock the Vote
http://www.rockthevote.com/

Search for Common Ground
http://www.sfcg.org/sfcg/sfcg_home.html

Society for International Development (SID)
http://www.sidint.org/

World Wildlife Foundation
http://www.worldwildlife.org/who/index.html

Street Law Inc.
http://www.streetlaw.org/en/Page.WhoWeAre.aspx

Streit Council
http://www.iaud.org/

Sunlight Foundation
http://www.sunlightfoundation.com/about/

Tax Payers Against Fraud
http://www.taf.org/abouttaf.htm

Third Way Center
http://www.thirdwaycenter.org/

Transparency International
http://www.transparency.org/about_us

Understanding Government
http://understandinggov.org/why/mission/

The United States Conference of Mayors
http://www.usmayors.org/

Victims of Communism Memorial Foundation
http://www.victimsofcommunism.org/about/

Vital Voices
http://www.vitalvoices.org/

Washington Foreign Law Society
http://www.wfls.org/version02/html/society.html

Women Empowered Against Violence, Inc. (WEAVE)
http://www.weaveincorp.org/about/

Women's Voices, Women's Vote
http://www.wvwv.org/

Woodrow Wilson Center for International Scholars
http://www.wilsoncenter.org/

Worldwatch Institute
http://www.worldwatch.org/

World Security Institute
http://www.worldsecurityinstitute.org/mission.cfm

World Organization for Human Rights- USA
http://www.humanrightsusa.org/

www.ingramcontent.com/pod-product-compliance
Lightning Source LLC
Chambersburg PA
CBHW080317290526
45790CB00005B/2076